HOW TO FIND YOUR INNER PRIESTESS

HOW TO FIND YOUR
⦿⦿⦿⦿ INNER ⦿⦿⦿⦿
PRIESTESS

KALA TROBE

HAY HOUSE
Australia – Canada – Hong Kong
South Africa – United Kingdom – United States

First published and distributed in the United Kingdom by Hay House UK Ltd,
Unit 62, Canalot Studios, 222 Kensal Rd, London W10 5BN.
Tel.: (44) 20 8962 1230; Fax: (44) 20 8962 1239.
www.hayhouse.co.uk

Published and distributed in the United States of America by Hay House, Inc.,
PO Box 5100, Carlsbad, CA 92018-5100.
Tel.: (1) 760 431 7695 or (800) 654 5126; Fax (1) 760 431 6948 or (800) 650 5115.
www.hayhouse.com

Published and distributed in Australia by Hay House Australia Ltd,
18/36 Ralph St, Alexandra NSW 2015.
Tel.: (61) 2 9669 4299; Fax: (61) 2 9669 4144.
www.hayhouse.com.au

Published and distributed in the Republic of South Africa by Hay House SA (Pty), Ltd,
PO Box 990, Witkoppen 2068.
Tel./Fax: (27) 11 706 6612.
orders@psdprom.co.za

Distributed in Canada by Raincoast,
9050 Shaughnessy St, Vancouver, BC V6P 6E5.
Tel.: (1) 604 323 7100; Fax: (1) 604 323 2600

A catalogue record for this book is available from the British Library.

ISBN 1-4019-0728-8

Printed and bound in Great Britain by TJ International, Padstow, Cornwall

Those through whom the spirit has once spoken
Are immortal and shall be remembered forever.

Epitaph of Maud Gonne, priestess extraordinaire

CONTENTS

Preface

The priestess abides in all of us, waiting to be found, worked with and realized. She represents the persona of optimum personal and spiritual potential. She is the Higher Self brought into everyday being. On this level she represents confidence, creativity, physical and spiritual energy and self-fulfilment, but the functions of a priestess are far more than simply personally relevant.

Though not exclusive to women, the arts of the priestess are feminist in nature, representing the full embodiment of the positive feminine and its dynamic and life-enhancing position in the evolving universe. The priestess therefore helps to quantum-leap humanity (as do all positive psycho-magickal practitioners), as well as living her 'own' life, as incarnated in individual consciousness, to its maximum potential.

Society in the West has reached a point at which the equality and in some cases superiority of the polar-feminine is being recognized and the repression of women on a mundane level is lessening by the day. Feminine spirituality is well and truly back and, like the priestesses who channel it, is here to stay. We still have a long way to go, but even the Church of England now includes women in its ministry. Admittedly,

the day when we'll see a female Pope is probably still far off, but in these cases we are dealing with outmoded and temporary patriarchal religions. They are the equivalent of the age of Ra before the Isian Era.*
(Words and phrases marked * in the text are explained in the Glossary; see page 191.)

Forget so-called 'political correctness', which has become toxic, poisoning the waters of reason with saccharine and guilt. Nobody should be judged by their race, religion or vital statistics, but on the grounds of their attitudes and actions towards others and themselves. If these are logically pernicious to women or to anyone else, or if the creeds are unbalanced and manipulative, then common sense alone dictates that they are to be avoided, and hopefully counteracted via spiritual mediation. Part of the job of the priestess is to re-dress the imbalance which has caused a topsy-turvy gender dynamic the world over and left the spirit of the planet – Nature – on her knees.

The priestess knows that the weighing of motive is the measure of Truth, just as it was in the Egyptian Hall of the Assessors. Here, the heart of the deceased would be weighed against the feather of Maat, Goddess of Justice, and even if trespasses had been committed, if the motive of the perpetrator was pure, the scales would balance and the soul would be admitted into the Underworld. If, however, the person was innately corrupt, then their heart would be devoured by the hideous monster Amut and their life-spark extinguished without honours. The modern priestess plays a similar symbolic role to that of the Goddess Maat. She is protector of Divine Truth, she works with integrity always, she judges others (if she must judge them at all) impartially and according to spiritual merit, and she is, above all, compassionate. She is not, however, hoodwinked by cultural trends of either tolerance or intolerance. She is her own judge, and her judgement is fair.

To bring these principles into a modern context, medieval-style doctrines of a patriarchal nature – I feel sure I don't need to name names – are unlikely to progress much as far as the liberation and equality of women are concerned. The tiny concessions that are occasionally made occur at a cosmic snail's pace. The priestess knows this and though her views are often attacked and vilified by bastions of the Old Path, she does not insult or deter others on their chosen or karmic paths, but neither does she accept insult or obstruction on her own chosen route. The priestess understands that the more women realize and release themselves as joyfully autonomous spiritual beings, the faster evolution will occur. Every woman who becomes a priestess, personally empowered as a representative of the divine feminine, serving the higher spiritual ideal, acting with moral conscience and enhancing the world around her, is speeding this process along. She also benefits personally, of course.

So, although this era has its restrictions, there are many advantages to it too. As well as social, political and religious progress for women, other wavelengths are beginning to affect planetary and personal consciousness. Despite the base energies of the Kali Yuga in which we abide, according to Hindu lore (a situation echoed in the philosophies of many other cultures), true Magick and ascension are almost as easy and possible as they were in lighter, more spiritual times. What a great era in which to be a priestess!

Acknowledgements

With special thanks to Michelle Pilley for helping formulate this book and to Lizzie Hutchins for making the edit such a breeze.

What Can Finding Your Inner Priestess Do for You?

There are cosmic, political and personal aspects to becoming an effective priestess. There are also as many types of priestess as there are types of Goddess, or her earthly representative, woman. Most of us are couched in archetypes, or are combinations of archetypes.

ARCHETYPAL PRIESTESSES

The clinical and intuitive psychology of archetypes has been explored by several authors, including Jean Shiroda Bolen and Jean Houston, a one-time student and assistant of the groundbreaking anthropologist Joseph Campbell. The recognition of archetypal traits that emerged from their work is indicative of the new awareness of thealogy (feminine theology) and is certainly applicable to the arts and crafts of the modern priestess, as we shall be exploring later.

This new exploration of archetypes, based on Jung's discovery of the collective unconscious, means that every possible genre of individual is able to consciously optimize their innate proclivities, as well as to actively explore other natural energy patterns and their cosmic representatives. For example, the new pattern of empathetic working presents voluptuous domestic Goddesses (and I don't simply mean Nigella Lawson, though she certainly is one!), Goddesses of science and intellect, fierce and passionate warrior Goddesses and, to cut a long story short, an ideal for anyone of any nature to aspire towards and represent. Needless to say, male equivalents of each blueprint are also out there.

Some people are a combination of archetypes, psychological chimeras with much innovative potential. Other people relate better to one direct energy pattern. Others still – and the priestess is usually adept at this – are able to move gracefully from one to another as circumstance dictates; that is, they are spiritual shape-shifters. This befits the shamanic cultures which originally informed the research of Campbell and his crew and has made a significant impact on modern psychology and spirituality.

One might call these archetypes 'cosmic role-models' and in my opinion that's precisely what we need in an era in which cosmetically-defined good looks are considered the ultimate Holy Grail for women, along with that old terrestrial bugbear, the acquisition of wealth and status. The priestess of course knows these concerns to be ephemeral, though it is true that if she possesses a quality or gift, she will enjoy it to the hilt, just as a Goddess of that property would wish her to. Its absence, however, is not mourned.

THE BODY: VEHICLE OF THE DIVINE

The fulfilment of social and personal aspirations is a core function of the priestess and we shall be exploring this later, through an intellectual study of the history of the priestess and through basic exercises to improve physical, psychological and spiritual well-being. All of these qualities are required of course and the body of the priestess truly is the temple of the Goddess.

This does not mean that luxuries cannot be enjoyed or indulgences permitted; on the contrary, the temples of the Goddesses of yore were often places of sensuality, hedonism and excess – but always in her name. There is a huge difference between committing an act in spiritual consciousness and doing it through habit or peer-pressure. This even applies to drinking alcohol or smoking a cigarette, for example; acts unequivocally frowned upon by some exponents of spirituality and New Age philosophy, yet many ancient priestesses were both inebriated and thoroughly fumigated in order to make them more receptive to the 'other'; that is, the Divine. The priestesses of Apollo, for example, were surrounded by laurel smoke and chewed the leaves too in the hope of gaining oracular powers. Alcohol, usually wine or mead, was so widely and habitually used that it barely requires a mention; indeed, before modern sanitation it was often the safest form of liquid to imbibe, as bacteria cannot live in it, as they can in unfermented drinks.

The priestess knows that 'pure is as pure does', and though she respects and cares for her body, she is not fanatical about its upkeep and knows when to cut herself a little slack and when to rein herself in.

Sexuality is also important to the priestess, though again it is neither a vice nor a necessity, rather a pleasure in the gifts of the Goddess and possibly an energy to use to enhance magickal and spiritual work (in the sacred art of Tantra, for example). Any decent historian knows how active with their sexuality many ancient priestesses were, at least on high days and holy days. What a contrast to the veiled nuns and women in burkhas created by the medieval religions! We will look a little at the raising of sensuality in the priestess later in this book.

THE PRIESTESS OF THE EARTH

There is another pressing issue, of which many priestesses are aware: that of the environment. Gaia-based priestesses and their empathizers are deeply concerned with the subject of environmental decline on this planet. The results of this empathy and concern have led to ritual workings to protect areas under threat, such as woods that are being bulldozed to make room for roads and car parks, and to counteracting environmental pollution on a wider scale. Other priestesses have striven to heal the nature devas in areas which have been assaulted and to enhance natural energies. This is very much the role modern Witchcraft and Wicca have performed. These revived thealogies have brought about the re-creation of environmentally-conscious priestesses and figureheads who are willing and able to channel positive energy into the Earth and its plants and creatures.

However, as author and witch Marion Green pointed out in a talk at the Witchcraft Seminar in Cornwall recently, it is not so much the Earth that needs healing as the people in it. Thus it might be more constructive to aim at increasing human awareness and curtailing human greed than focusing on the self-replenishing Earth, which has nothing innately wrong with it. The priestess is in a prime position to perform such a task. Let's work together to change the world!

Some priestesses do not relate specifically to the Earth; we also have lunar, solar and stellar representatives here. The Maatian priestess Nema *(see Recommended Reading)* is one example of a modern magickal priestess who, though it is impossible to sum her up in a nutshell, and at the risk of sounding like something out of *Star Trek*, clearly comprehends the inter-dimensional stellar realms beyond the Earth plane. This might be succinctly translated as 'the consciousness of other galaxies'. This unlikely-seeming quality is the mark of any advanced modern (and indeed, ancient) priestess, as you will discover during your own explorations of inner and outer space.

So, on a larger scale, the priestess represents the bridge between this spiritual aeon and the next. It is obvious to those with psychic abilities that a dramatic transition is occurring at present, often referred to as the 'New Age' or 'Age of Aquarius'. This is the preliminary stage to a universal raising of consciousness and eventual ascension into a more spiritually evolved level.

Now, whether the location of the 'New Age' for humanity and its affiliates will be this planet is debatable. Many pagans would argue the affirmative, that we are children of this Earth and should not be so ungrateful as to wish to leave our mother. Gratitude for many of us is not the issue, as clearly we love it on Earth – why else would we have evolved here? We do indeed have much to be thankful for in this conducive and naturally beautiful environment. Most esotericists, Hindus and Buddhists, however, would consider the pending elevation to be literal, if not physical. In death, we progress to the astral and causal spheres, or 'the afterlife', or 'heaven or hell', if you find these terms more palatable. Either way, we are capable of existing in other spheres and dimensions, with more refined (less material) wavelengths and thought processes and points of reference very different from those of Earth.

Whichever standpoint we take, it goes without saying that we have a duty to leave this welcoming planet in good and natural condition. Also, however the individual priestess interprets the spiritual evolution of the species, she will act as its ingress to this level.

THE PERSONAL PATH OF THE PRIESTESS

We can already see that the work of the priestess is much more than a personal path. But let us look briefly at some of the personal repercussions of the many arts of the priestess.

The sort of manifestations we might reasonably expect on this level are various, but they are always empowering. For the sporty woman – the runner, for example – the inner priestess can have very tenable results, such as facilitating peak performance (especially with the help of Artemis!). For the creative priestess, it can represent easy interaction with the Muse (who is, of course, the Goddess) and the production of new and inspired works of art, literature and music, to name but a few. For the woman working daily and getting stuck on public transport (most of us go through this mundane equation at some point or other, usually often), accessing of the priestess within represents the star of hope and aspiration. During this stage of gradual initiation, we know what we wish to achieve and in which direction to aim. The night is dark, as it is in the realms of dense matter, but we follow the divine luminary. Yes, we stumble along the way, for it is never easy to follow the star, but at least we know where we want to go, and can keep our eye fixed on the long-term goal despite temporary tribulation.

Essentially, the art of the priestess is magickal in that it represents the manifestation of Will. The focused priestess can achieve just about anything, whatever her mundane situation may be.

ARE PRIESTESSES BORN OR MADE?

It is interesting to contemplate whether a priestess is born or made. As I see it, all women have the potential to become priestesses. Many women act in a priestess-like manner without ever calling it such; perhaps they lack the spiritual referents to name the process. Examples are women who have fought their way in political circles, who stand up for what they believe at all costs and who try to improve conditions for others. We will be looking at some of these role-models in the next chapter, to give ourselves a firm grounding in our historical roots. Perhaps these women might be classified as 'natural priestesses'. By following their True Will, they are self-made priestesses, or living representatives and enhancers of particular energies.

It is my personal belief, however, that some religious priestesses are born. For example, those of us who tend naturally towards Magick and thealogy from childhood, those of us who are fascinated by ancient pantheons such as Egyptian and Hindu, or who veer toward what is commonly called witchcraft. Such women are usually re-incarnations of former priestesses (who will no doubt have lived many less illustrious lives between then and now). This is partly down to the fact that many of us took vows of service to Deity in former lives, and of course this service never ends, no matter how times change.

As ours is a potent era of spiritual development, it makes sense that many of the Old Ones are coming back to aid the birth of the new aeon. Also, it is a fact that there are more people alive on the planet today than ever before – quite a vertiginous statistic. Viewed through the philosophy of re-incarnation, this must mean that there are many Old Ones here as well as the new souls which arrive in every era.

If you are a priestess born, you will most likely be intuitive, perhaps even telepathic or psychic. You will be naturally concerned about the 'greater things in life' – that is, political and spiritual overviews. You will be naturally compassionate and almost certainly inclined toward the mystical. You may even have access to long-term memories – dreams which are startlingly life-like and perhaps retrospective, flashes of the distant past and other consciousnesses, proclivities you cannot logically explain (for example, you were born and raised in Barnsley by atheist parents, but have a passionate attraction to Eskimo or Assyrian mythology and religion!).

I do not believe regression to be necessarily of use – after all, it is the present which is the point of power – but if it occurs naturally or during magickal training or activity, the information gleaned can put fuel in the priestess's rocket, so to speak, even if simply as a resurgent (some might say atavistic) energy link.

EXPRESSING THE GODDESS

On a wider scale, a major role of the priestess is, as I heard one talented esotericist put it, 'to shut up and give the Goddess the chance to speak'. A danger of the early stages of finding your inner priestess, or indeed of any magickal and much spiritual work, is the belief in one's talent and unique connection to the Divine to such an extent that it becomes megalomania. Many priestesses in the early stages of their explorations begin to confuse themselves with the Goddess. Yes, of course you are her representative, but as such you are her vessel, and adoration should be focused on the hidden Divine, not the mortal representing it.

This devotion requires a sort of wantonness in the priestess; the ability to receive information and interaction on an insatiable basis. There's no point in attuning to the free-flowing Goddess at 6 o'clock if you're definitely going to break off at 7.30 to watch *Coronation Street*. Accessing the inner priestess requires ongoing work and true commitment.

It goes without saying that the intuitive faculties need to be maintained and developed as if one were an athlete training the body for the

Olympics. The discipline required is not mere persistence; it is also the control of the lower nature, especially the emotional body.

Being an effective priestess, especially if you are working in a group, also requires the ability to mimic astral and spiritual forms, hence the name given to Helena Blavatsky, the founder of Theosophy,* and to priestesses in general: 'The Ape of Thoth' (Thoth being the Egyptian god of esoteric lore, Magick and divination). The reproduction of certain energies helps to empower them on a tangible plane. Many of the best priestesses who have served the gods and humanity hitherto have been trained actresses, singers and dancers. Traditional temple priestesses were expert in reproducing gesture, dance, voice and facial expression to perfectly reflect the deity they were serving. This ancient art may still be witnessed in *Katha Nritya*, the art practised by Hindu Kathak dancers in which the God or Goddess being worshipped is mimicked via *tala* (rhythm), *mudra* (gesture), *karana* (posture) and *bhava* (expression). Through this process, the dancers actually *become* the Goddess or God.

Few of us nowadays in the West, with its inhibited physicality and gracelessness, will be able to reproduce the qualities of the Goddess so flawlessly. However, there is much that may be done on a number of other levels, as the following chapters will show.

The Priestess in History:
Our Role-Models

As modern priestesses, we will be (or already are) carrying the torch of various spiritual and sociological principles. What we do may well be innovative, but it is never self-generated, for we are treading a path much-travelled, and were it not for this fact, we would become stuck in brambles very swiftly.

An empirical understanding of the route is a preliminary any sensible traveller will undertake. So, let us take a swift aerial overview of the path of the modern priestess so that we may assess the lie of the land and give due thanks at the various shrines scattered along the way.

It is said that behind every great man there has to be a great woman. I would extend this observation to the fact that behind every great movement – spiritual, political and cultural – there is at least one powerful priestess, and often several.

In this chapter we will look at the role of the priestess and at some of the women who have influenced the world as we know it today. Then we will explore how to bring out the priestess within – the full manifestation of the Higher Self and one's personal and spiritual potential.

THE CRAFT OF THE PRIESTESS IN THE WEST

Historically speaking, a priestess is a girl or woman whose life is dedicated to the service of a particular deity. This involves performing the tasks relevant to that God or Goddess, such as tending their temple and altar, performing rites of cleanliness and sometimes undertaking specific roles such as divination and devotional ritual. She is also an intermediary between the divine and the mortal, a living gateway or bridge between the worlds. So, traditionally, the priestess is a focal point for concentrated spiritual and magickal energy. This is a function mostly, though not exclusively, performed by the female. However, some men also carry Goddess energy and are capable of performing some priestess functions.

Mythology and archaeology reveal to us many of the old functions of the priestess. Ancient literature, such as *The Odyssey* and *The Iliad*, does the same. However, the craft of the priestess dropped out of recorded history in the West, or was abandoned altogether, thanks to the infiltration of new and highly patriarchal religions. It was revived centuries later, mainly through the influence of Theosophy and then the Golden Dawn,* during the Victorian era, when there was a massive upsurge of interest in myth, folklore and Magick, as there always is when a woman is on the throne.

Let us look at Great Britain, which after all is widely recognized in modern spirituality as the home of the Grail of mystical truth.

Elizabeth I was a patron of the arts magickal and we find traces of the priestess's craft in Elizabethan literature as well as many references to the magickal and fairy realms. Even the date of Elizabeth's coronation was determined by her court astrologer and alchemist, John Dee, with the help of his visionary, Edward Kelley, who in this context was performing the role once performed by women dedicated to the sacred.

Of course, in those days the occult arts were perceived as a respectable science, part of every Renaissance gentleman's repertoire of skills, and logical in nature. It has only been since the industrial revolution and the publishing of Charles Darwin's *The Origin of Species* that logos, appropriated by the atheist and Christian alike, has become the self-declared enemy of the intuitive faculties in certain scenarios. Rather ironic, as these faculties were in ancient times ascribed to Goddesses such as the Egyptian Maat and the Greek Athena, the cerebral child of Zeus. However, until recently they have been appropriated by men, at least in the Western Hemisphere.

Unfortunately, history casts a thealogical blank over the next few centuries, as most of the records were made by scholars and the only educated and accepted creeds came, again, from men trained in this blinkered way of thinking. So our aerial view becomes a little obfuscated as we fly over the priestess's chronological path and arrive in the eighteenth century. We can, however, rest assured that many of the traditions continued, perpetuated by strong women of all creeds and social statuses, either through the power of archetype working within them (there is no getting away from the blueprint of the Goddess!) or through conscious recognition of the Divine in nature.

The occult arts suddenly flourished again under Queen Victoria. We have a rich fund of writing, painting and music to affirm this. Even the Poet Laureate, Lord Alfred Tennyson, was deeply preoccupied by myth and legend, and many of his poems revolve around Goddess-related characters such as Guinevere, Aurora, the Greek Goddess of dawn, and other mystical personae. This trend is also apparent in the works of other popular and enduring writers of the time: Keats, the Shelleys,

Christina Rossetti (in whose poem 'Goblin Market' two Goddess-like sisters are severely compromised by an unpleasant and invasive masculine principle) and of course Samuel Taylor Coleridge. Paintings of the time redoubled the emphasis on feminine-based spirituality, mainly through the works of the Pre-Raphaelites. Admittedly, many of the female characters in these paintings appear as victims, but they are also sublime and impassive, and often deified, such as Circe, who 'raises her cup to Ulysses' in Hunt's wonderful painting. The lifting of the veil was at hand under the female monarch, even though Victoria's participation in the revival may be safely categorized as inadvertent.

As we will explore in a moment, this cultural outflux of hidden Goddess spirituality was largely a symptom of what was going on in the populace at large, for good art always reflects a particular cultural and spiritual process. Interest in the afterlife was at an all-time high. People of the middle and upper classes had just enough effective medication to stop them dying before they had explored at least a little of the Mysteries. Tables were tapped, séances held, and in England and America Spiritualism re-emerged. This has continued to hold the imagination and aspirations of society ever since and the Goddess has been reborn into modern consciousness. With her, of course, come her priestesses.

These ancient arts have resurfaced most noticeably under the current queen, Elizabeth II. This is partly down to social evolution of course, but it is interesting to look at the symbolism behind her role. The Queen is the tangible Shakti* of the people, as the Grail mythos attests, in that a true monarch in the Gnostic Grail tradition is given service of the Chalice through the fact that they, the people and the land are one, and so they are 'possessed' by the divine spirit that serves the Grail. That they are aware of this is not required, thankfully.

In ancient times the regent was well aware of their divine role and was subsequently revered as a deity, or a manifestation of Spirit. Because of corruption caused by megalomania in various figureheads, this role is no longer spiritually tenable, though the monarch may well act as an unconscious spectrum through which divine energies are passed and magnified in different rays or wavelengths. In the contemporary era, we can each become one of these foci through knowledge, intent, meditation and practice of the ancient magickal arts. So the priestess serves the same function as the monarch, in a cosmic sense.

Let us continue our flight over the terrain of progressive spirituality. Since the 1960s, the upsurge of thealogy and the shift away from orthodox religions into a freer form of spiritual expression, plus the recent popularity of paganism and Witchcraft, have brought a new breed of priestess to light.

Wicca,* which has infiltrated the 'alternative religion' scene since the 1970s, has played an important role in precipitating the return of the role of the priestess. The modern religion of Wicca is the thought-child of ancient paganism combined with comparatively recent feminism. The most obvious active forms of expression of the Goddess are the well-versed rituals of 'Drawing Down the Moon' and 'Assuming the Goddess Form', both of which we will be looking at later in this book. The assumption of the form of the Goddess involves channelling and 'becoming' a particular deity, and is a key technique to Wiccan practice. This is not quite the same as the rites of possession in Voodoo ritual, as the effects of working in this way are less visceral and much more subtle nowadays. In Ancient Egypt, the rituals were heavily influenced by the African diasporic cults, from which Voodoo originates, and were consequently more physical, that being the energy required at the time.

However, Wicca and Witchcraft have helped to bring this method of working directly with divinity once more to the fore, and its effects are psychically palpable. The energies being delivered into the realms of matter have changed. More lunar current is reaching us – a wavelength that facilitates the psychic and intuitive arts, access to the subconscious and Magick itself. The rise of interest in Goddess studies and the research of authors such as Joseph Campbell into archetypes have also 'upped the voltage', so to speak. The modern world, particularly the Western world, has become a potent network of psycho-spiritual energies. The priestess is their channel and their mouthpiece.

Channelling, which became popular in the Victorian era following the groundbreaking work of Helena Blavatsky and the spread of Theosophy and Spiritualism, has also played a significant role in the return of priest- and priestess-related craft.

Channelling began mainly through the delivering of books to 'psychic secretaries' on the Earth plane, as Alice Bailey put it. She was the channel for 'the Tibetan Master'. The Theosophical belief in Hidden Masters – that is, guardians and guides of human evolution who exist on the inner planes – hugely affected this trend. It became the task of the sensitive to record their messages as accurately as possible. Some works of astonishing complexity, sometimes containing languages and skills unknown to the 'secretary', have been delivered in this manner.

The latter-day developments of this channelling are clearly visible everywhere in the 'alternative spirituality' scene. The role of psychic secretary, greatly akin to that of the ancient priestess, has been keenly adopted by a large sector of individuals, and their contacts are no less various. A brief glance at any New Age magazine will now reveal those claiming to be in touch with everything from inter-stellar intelligences to the dolphin spirits of Sirius to Angels. Obviously it is necessary to use personal intuition and discrimination to deduce which are real and which deluded. However, the revival of this practice, which is somewhat akin to the role of the Delphic and other ancient oracles, has done much to revive the pertinence of the one acting as priestess.

We now have to deflect from our aerial route a little and fly eastward, towards India and Tibet.

THE EASTERN INFLUENCE

Another important influence on occidental occult development and the role of the female has come to us from complementary ancient civilizations. The Theosophists introduced much Eastern technique and terminology into their work, not to mention belief in concepts such as the Akashic Records, an astral repository for all that has ever been conceptualized or experienced, rather akin to Jung's collective unconscious, but with great *magickal* import.

Hinduism, Buddhism and oriental practices such as Tai Chi and Zen have also affected the psychic atmosphere. Before this, the only modern representative of feminine spirituality in the West was Mary, 'Mother of God', a role of martyrdom and pietà – Mary of Sorrow, the Virgin, the passive, Isis as the Goddess of mourning only, stripped of her power to fructify. Strong Goddesses such as Bride and Freya of the Celtic and Norse mythos were not tenably present until the revival of paganism over recent decades. Qabalistically* related to the sephirah Binah, Mary, 'Mother of God', describes an important function, that of restriction into form, but this is just one of many facets of the Goddess. Modern priestess-craft allows *all* aspects to be explored and represented. We can be wise, and feisty, and fertile, and powerful in all senses.

The potent Goddesses of Hinduism have become vivid and much-needed female role-models in the West; many a Western priestess will mention Kali and Durga, for example, as primary Goddess forms.

To swoop in on our trail a little more closely, the Tantric Vama-Marg*
Current contains the most refined forms of the priestess arts that are
known to exist, to the extent that mantras (chants) delineate the sound-
vectors of the manifestation of the Goddess's body-mind, and the cor-
responding yantras represent her visible form and power. Yantras are
diagrams often carved into copper (though not necessarily), which
represent the geometric shapes of certain energies contained within
various Goddesses. These are meditated on by adepts, along with
appropriate mantra and *bhakti* (devotional ritual), in order to evoke the
blessings and energies of the Goddess concerned. We will be looking
at some of these Goddesses later in the book and at how the less initiated priest or priestess might approach them!

In the meantime, it is interesting to note that only the *female* deities have
yantras, because they represent form – as in, again, Binah, Qabalistically
speaking – symbolizing restriction. However, this 'restriction' is much
more empowered than that of the Catholic Goddess, as we shall see.

Certain Tantric sects don't use a yantra as a gateway of the Goddess,
but use the yoni of the priestess as the means of her manifestation.
Hinduism, the exoteric version of Tantra, has perpetuated the idea of
the devotee as a direct interface with the Goddess.

In India, every married woman loyal to her husband and family is a
devotee of Sita, the divine epitome of the perfect consort, and is her living priestess. Admittedly, Sita's role as a Goddess is very much male-
orientated, as she represents the Perfect Wife. The theme of self-sacrifice
is controversial, but it cannot be ignored that here the 'ordinary
woman' directly emulates the Goddess. The same pantheon, however,
contains chaste Goddesses (Durga), bloody and vengeful Goddesses
(Kali), possessively craving but emotionally comprehensible Goddesses
(Radha), Goddesses of wisdom (Sarasvati) and sensual, beneficent
feminine deities (Laxmi).

The idea of deity as role-model is not exclusive to Eastern religions, but it is obvious that a pantheon which contains female as well as male deities, each with his or her own tincture and boons, will better furnish the general populace both spiritually and psychologically. The ancients of every single religion realized this and gave a fair share of attention to both male and female deities. Christianity and Islam, in contrast, have little or no reverence for the female divine. Also of import to the role of the modern priestess is contemporary interest in Buddhism, particularly Tibetan Buddhism, and the role of meditation on particular Gods and Goddesses as epitomes of specific energies.

These Eastern influences were tied in with Western occult and religious practice by the great Theosophical priestess Helena Blavatsky. She in turn influenced the innovative magickal school called the Golden Dawn, which actively included (indeed, required) priestesses in its rituals. We need to take a much closer look at this school in order to truly understand our history and role as priestesses today, as it has influenced us vastly, and in a very understated way.

SOME PRIESTESSES OF THE PAST

The Golden Dawn was founded in London in 1887. It consisted almost entirely of the highly intelligent, educated and creative élite and soon listed amongst its members the poet W. B. Yeats and the tea heiress Annie Horniman, whose family created museums still extant today. The Golden Dawn worked myth, Magick and syncretism into the spiritual wavelengths of London and Paris particularly, in a gender-balanced manner. The role of women as priestesses was key to the enduring influence of this one-time obscure group, which has hugely influenced modern Witchcraft, arguably the most visible Goddess cult of the present day.

Let us look at some specific women who influenced this group and then at the Golden Dawn initiates themselves and what they did on a practical level that still affects us. We will have to swoop and swerve a little, but any priestess, like Isis in her bird-form seeking Osiris, will become adept at this.

Going right back, we have legendary women such as Morgana, whose mythos has permeated the ages. The figures of Cerridwen, the Celtic sorceress, and various ancient Goddesses have infused history and folklore to such an extent that we can list any magickal female featured in them as a descendent of the Goddess and a sort of priestess in that she evokes in our minds the allegories which speak of the feminine divine. Celtic and Gaelic folklore underwent a vast revival in the eighteenth century and was keenly explored by the priestesses of the Golden Dawn.

To leave the Emerald Isle for a moment, we find another well-known representative of the Goddess in the arid but magickally fertile land of Egypt. Cleopatra was an active priestess considered to be divine by her people. Her Magick and glamour still captivate our imagination so strongly that many magickally-minded people seem to believe they actually *were* her!

Joan of Arc was a warrior priestess canonized by the French, even though she broke every rule in the 'good Catholic girl's handbook'. Her simplicity and purity – she was known to the French as *La Pucelle,* the Virgin – instantly align her to deities such as Artemis and Athena, as does her martial role. She became a French national icon, symbolically echoed in Britain by the figure 'Britannia', who also bears a striking resemblance to Athena. I think we can safely deduce that both figures fulfil a role once played by the Roman Goddesses who merged with the local deities of Britain and France. In both cases, we witness a female figurehead who evokes inspiration and loyalty to a cause (primary tasks of the priestess) and whose role is simultaneously sublime and practical.

Now let us look at some more recent women who forged the way for the modern priestess, consciously or not.

Honing in on the nineteenth century, we find the unlikely name of Marie Curie. Why do I mention her? You may well wonder. First, because she was one of the women who demonstrated that the female brain, rather than being the feeble and fanciful thing men had ordained it to be, was actually a rather more complex organ and one capable of great advancement even in the – gasp! – male-only field of science. Secondly, I mention Marie Curie because, by discovering the first radio-active isotope, she was the original receptacle of the concept of nuclear power and therefore the Shakti* of the atomic era. Now whether this was a good thing or not is another matter. But she did forge her way for compassion's sake and simply through intellectual ability in the academic and cerebral worlds, making her symbolically a priestess of Athena.

On a more obviously *magickal* level, we find witch Paterson, the literal priestess and initiator of artist and esotericist Austin Osman Spare.* She was an old lady who apparently had the ability to shape-shift into a beautiful young girl. This of course is a time-honoured tradition among witches and priestesses. Spare himself was fascinated by the Crone aspect of the Goddess, as we can see from his many sketches and paintings of various 'hags'. One of his favourite models was actually 93 years of age. Witch Paterson claimed descent from a line of Salem witches who had managed to escape Cotton Mather's* persecutions. She acted as Austin Spare's initiator, Muse and priestess. Spare's work bridges the gap between Hermetic Magick and Witchcraft and has provided us with one of the most primeval forms of Witchcraft known today – atavistic resurgence – which of course has led us eventually to Chaos Magick.* Had this aesthetically-challenging old colonial lady not seduced Spare in all senses, the magickal world we inhabit today would be very different.

Talking of artists, another witchy woman who hugely influenced modern art was Gala Dali, wife of Salvador. The Surrealists, like many of the Pre-Raphaelites, had an active interest in the arts magickal and it was Gala who encouraged her husband to explore the occult arts. She also acted as his Muse and his priestess. In Dali's novel *Hidden Faces (see Recommended Reading)*, which I very much recommend as part of magickal studies, several key magickal and Tantric techniques are described. Gala also had a pervasive influence on other key writers and painters of that era, such as Paul Eluard, to whom she was originally married, and Max Ernst.

The Influence of the Golden Dawn Priestesses

Many of our most powerful priestesses have been highly educated and intellectual, as well as 'hands on' and political, and hopefully the same applies today. The priestess performs the sacred function of *pontiff*, thus part of her role is to pontificate – she acts as a bridge between human and divine intelligences, as does a priest, or, in Roman Catholic terms, the Pope. The Delphic Oracle did exactly the same thing.

The women of the Golden Dawn were perfect examples of priestesses – they were feminists, humanitarians, political movers and shakers, highly creative, and they experimented with consciousness in a way that has saturated spirituality as we know it today. For example, the colours we ascribe to the sephiroth* on the Tree of Life came from the palette of Moina Mathers, who was an artist as well as the first initiate of the Golden Dawn. They simply happened to be the shades of paint available at that time – though of course the actual colours were perceived psychically.

Such details aside, these women were alive at a time when the role of the cultured female was perceived to be staying at home and being demure. All of the women of the Golden Dawn were fiercely self-defining, and indeed the founders of the Order were avid supporters of the suffragettes and female liberation, even the old Masonic codgers like William Westcott, one of its founders. So their influence permeated many layers of society, including the political, and they were key reformers who were certainly not shy of taking the platform.

Included in the original Golden Dawn were the Fenian political activist Maud Gonne; Annie Horniman, artist, thespian and heiress to a fortune; Moina Bergson Mathers, whom Annie had met at the Slade School of Art; the talented actress Florence Farr; Constance Wilde, the highly unsung wife of Oscar; and Pamela Colman Smith, artist and designer of the Rider-Waite Tarot deck.

Maud Gonne

Maud Gonne was in my opinion one of the most amazing priestesses ever to walk this Earth, so we are going to take a good look at this stately impassioned woman as she wonders around her beloved Ireland and as she coheres her love of the land and its people with the arts of the priestess.

She began her incarnation in 1866 as the daughter of a wealthy army officer of Irish descent and an English mother, who died when Maud was two. She was educated by a governess in France and spent most of her childhood flitting between France and Ireland. She became devoted to Irish independence after witnessing various injustices in her childhood – such as a woman lying near a ditch starving to death and the English landlord commenting that he hoped she got on with it soon, she was spoiling the view – and in 1900 she founded the Daughters of Erin, a revolutionary women's society. Their attitude was practical.

For example, they arranged for 30,000 Irish schoolchildren to be diverted from a celebration to welcome Queen Victoria on a trip to Ireland by holding a gigantic free picnic.

With Ella Young* and several members of the Golden Dawn, including William Butler Yeats, Maud attempted to bring back the old ways to Ireland. She used Witchcraft techniques to contact the spirits of the dead and the spirits of the land in order to liberate Ireland from British rule. The peasants spoke of her as 'Daughter of the Sidhe', a fairy-woman sent to free them. She was incredible looking – over six feet tall, slim, with long burnished hair and eyes that were described as strangely 'golden'. A Pre-Raphaelite dream no doubt, and her glamour was used to amplify her voice as a priestess. Like all of the women of the Golden Dawn, she was experimental with her looks as well as her Magick, favouring long dramatic gowns and theatrical garb, except for when she was on her revolutionary lecture tours and staying in the hovels of peasants, when I imagine she dressed down somewhat.

Like many magickal women, Maud Gonne was respected but widely feared and vilified by men, and sometimes women, who hated to see a liberated female. She was often accused of such idiocies as devil-worship by those who failed to understand the purity and holiness of natural energies. In 1918 she was actually arrested in Dublin and, without charge, interned in London's Holloway jail for six months, which one can guess was even worse then than it would be now. She nearly died of pulmonary tuberculosis as a result.

The Victorian priestesses also had another danger to contend with. If their families suspected them of magickal activity or other perceived deviance, they could have them imprisoned like Maud, or committed for insanity. Annie Horniman was directly blackmailed by a male rival in the Golden Dawn who threatened to write to her father and tell him of her activities in a 'Witchcraft cult', so that she would be put in an asylum. Luckily she pointed out that he would have a time of it trying to explain in court what 'magick' really was – and of course that's why the Witchcraft Act was eventually repealed, because nobody believed in it or wanted to admit that it existed. However, Annie was lucky; many other magickally talented women were not.

Of course, being imprisoned or committed was simply the contemporary version of the old witch trials, with their torturings, duckings, hangings and burnings. How fortunate we are to live in the modern era and in hemispheres where such injustices are defunct! Equivalent practices are still carried out by Middle Eastern religions and societies, however.

Maud managed to survive her imprisonment, though only just. She regained her strength and continued to be the educated, politically aware, theatrical woman she was: a classic Golden Dawn priestess. Her magickal motto, which translates as 'Through Fire to the Light', is reminiscent of the fires of Beltane* – and Maud did much to help reinstate the ancient festivals in Ireland. The motto shows her willingness to face pain and necessary transmuting processes, and of course it reflects her will to *fight*.

Yeats was obsessed with her all of his life and they shared an intense long-term friendship, during which Maud acted as his poetical and magickal muse. Here again, we see the priestess as the inspiring force behind great literature, art and political movements. Maud and Yeats were married on the spiritual planes in a mutual dream, but Maud refused to marry him on this level, preferring, she said, 'men of action' to poets. It is likely that she did not wish to destroy their magickal magnetism by dissipating it via physical interaction, a subject that Dion Fortune discusses at length in her books on occult arts *(see Recommended Reading)*. So instead they experimented with Qabalistic Magick, revivals of ancient rites, particularly Celtic, astral projection, and many other activities we take for granted in modern esoteric practice.

It is bemusing to read biographies of Maud Gonne or William Butler Yeats which neglect to mention this aspect of their lives – and there are several that try to ignore or gloss over their magickal interests – as they were of vast importance to them.

As well as actively participating in Witchcraft and high magickal ritual, Maud was constantly having prophetic dreams and was adept at divination. During the First World War she worked with the Red Cross ten hours a day tending the injured and dying in France in horrendous conditions. She 'pontificated' on a frequent basis – i.e. literally got onto platforms to speak at rallies and political events – but she was never scared to get her hands dirty. She sold all of her jewellery to feed the starving and had an extremely hands-on approach to what we might call 'practical Magick'.

Maud lived a long, fruitful and often excruciating life until 1953 – and, as her epitaph says, 'Those through whom the Spirit has spoken are Immortal and shall live forever.' This phrase epitomizes the oracular aspects of the arts of the priestess.

Annie Horniman

Another major priestess in the early Golden Dawn was Annie Horniman. She cut an unusual figure in Victorian England by chain-smoking cigarettes, riding a bike whilst wearing bloomers – which no woman *ever* did – and choosing not to marry. She was able to do this because she was independently wealthy. She provided much of the financial backing for the Golden Dawn and originally furnished the founders Moina and Samuel Mathers with a living wage for their magickal work. She met Moina at the Slade School of Art and they became firm friends. She was on the scene when Moina met Samuel in the Egyptian section of the British Museum and was privy to the first rays of the Golden Dawn. She later became its secretary. She performed one of the world's most famous Tarot readings, known as the Abbey Theatre reading, for W. B. Yeats, about the Irish National Theatre. She led a vivid and chequered career in the Order, undergoing expulsions, reinstatements and some terrible arguments, but she also worked some nifty Magick within the group.

Moina Mathers

Arguably the most important priestess of the Golden Dawn was its first initiate. Moina Mathers was born Mina Bergson in 1865. Even in childhood she was a talented artist with strong spiritual leanings. She went to the Slade School of Art just down the road from the British Museum and there met Samuel MacGregor Mathers, who spent most of his time in the reading rooms translating the grimoires.* There was an instant magickal rapport between Samuel and Mina, and they soon became priest and priestess in the astral worlds and husband and wife in the mundane one. It is highly likely that their marriage was physically chaste in order to increase its magickal productivity.

In 1888 Mina became the first initiate of the Golden Dawn. She was joined in 1890 by Annie Horniman, Florence Farr and Maud Gonne. Mina changed her name to the more Celtic-sounding Moina and dedicated herself to the Order, to supporting her husband in his role as its head and to aiding him in and sometimes illustrating his translations of magickal manuscripts, such as that of Abra-Melin the Mage.*

Perhaps the best-known and most fun thing about Moina and Samuel is that they performed the Rites of Isis publicly on stage in Paris, first in 1899 at the Théâtre Bodinière and then in 1900 at the World Fair centennial, where Samuel had been commissioned to create an Isis Temple, terrifying the locals with both the authenticity of the construction and the rituals that went on in it. One journalist actually fainted, which is hardly surprising as this 'side-show' was 100 per cent real

Magick being run by the heads of the Golden Dawn. It must have been something indeed.

Moina lived long after her husband's death and continued to play a very major role in the Order. Unfortunately for us, she was scrupulous about 'leaving no trace' – a principle echoed by her magickal motto – 'No Stepping Back' or 'Never to Retrace my Steps' – and burnt her private papers prior to her death, so less detail is known about her than about any of the other priestesses.

Florence Farr

When the actress Florence Farr was 30, she took the part of the priestess Amaryllis in the play *A Sicilian Idyll*. It took place under a Full Moon. The priestess played by Florence invokes the Moon Goddess Selene to destroy her errant lover. Both George Bernard Shaw and William Butler Yeats were in attendance and both fell in love with Florence's luminous beauty and unique thespian abilities. Shaw wanted her to be the main actress for his plays, though he had very specific ideas about oracular style, which they later argued over constantly, and Yeats considered her to be the only person capable of properly reciting his poetry. Florence practised a very particular art of oration, which was frequently utilized in her magickal rituals. In due course she became involved with both men professionally and with Yeats magickally. With Annie Horniman's financial aid, she gave both writers their first opportunity to produce stage plays. Naturally, they both wrote the leading parts for her.

Florence Farr's interest for us doesn't lie so much with her Golden Dawn activities or her work as an actress and sybil, though these are certainly to be admired, but as the founder of the Sphere Group, an offshoot of the Golden Dawn. The Sphere Group performed highly imaginative magickal workings, such as each person envisaging themselves as a sephirah on the Tree of Life and unifying, projecting gradually upwards until they were outside the Milky Way and channelling positive energy back to Earth, or performing astral explorations of the Enochian alphabet. Florence was also one of the four magickians who, in 1896, invoked the Spirit Taphthartharath (a mercurial spirit) to visible manifestation.

This kind of work, which the modern priestess approaches as an already-trodden path, would not be possible today had people like Florence, Annie, Moina and Maud not hacked away at the psychic and sociological undergrowth for us. Each of them certainly has a shrine by the astral wayside, just as ancient Goddesses such as Hecate and Minerva had literal ones.

Florence was highly innovative and a great organizer of ritual workings. She orated, she taught, she wrote several books, and the part she played in the early Golden Dawn was considerable. At the age of 52 she left London for Ceylon, where she ended her days teaching at a girls' school and no doubt spreading much love and wisdom around her, as reflected by her magickal motto, 'Wisdom is a Gift given to the Wise.'

Pamela Colman Smith and Dion Fortune

Pamela Colman Smith, or 'Pixie', as she was known, is a somewhat unsung artist and priestess. She designed the amazing Rider-Waite Tarot deck, which has been the main influence in Tarot design and usage in the modern era, and for which she was apparently paid an absolute pittance. She had a strong relationship with the elemental realms and a highly idiosyncratic personality. If she was still alive, she would doubtlessly be honoured as a living representative of the Goddess – probably of the Muses and the elemental deities such as the Naiads. Personally, I use her cards just about every day. The Golden

Dawn employed them as portals to specific wavelengths and correspondences, and the Rider-Waite (referred to by some feminists as 'the
Smith-Rider deck') is particularly good for that.

However, probably the most popular and best-known priestess from
the era is Dion Fortune. Her Society of the Inner Light* nickname was
'Fluff', because she used to pick the bits of fluff off the carpet when
they all shared a homestead. I have often thought it inappropriate that
people refer to vagueness in New Age and Witchcraft-related philosophies as 'fluff' or 'fluffiness', considering that 'Fluff' Fortune was one of
the most hardcore dedicated occultists of her time.

Dion's contribution to occult literature and understanding is vast.
Her novels, such as *Moon Magic, The Winged Bull* and *The Sea
Priestess*, still work in a contemporary context, although some of her
non-fiction writings don't quite, such as *The Problem of Purity*, which
she wrote under her real name of Violet Firth, in which she endorses
chastity at all costs – but she was writing very much in her era, which
was by nature restrictive. However, *The Mystical Qabalah* remains in
my opinion the best book on the Qabalah of the Western Mystery
Tradition ever written and *Psychic Self-Defence* is an absolute classic
and is considered by many to be the definitive book on the subject.
Dion's common sense and descriptive prose are unrivalled.

She was initiated into the Golden Dawn in 1919 as 'Deo, non
Fortuna', meaning 'By God, not by Chance'. By this point her psychic
and magickal abilities were already well developed. She seems, however, to have become caught up in the petty backbiting and general
paranoia that plagued the Golden Dawn (the old version of contemporary 'Bitchcraft and Bicca', the bane of many working groups), as she
suspected Moina Mathers of attacking her psychically. Whether this
was true or not is impossible to tell, and it seems to me rather unlikely, though Moina certainly went through many personal challenges

during her incarnation. Both of the Mathers were admittedly inclined to accuse people of not having the correct symbols in their auras and so forth, and Moina definitely *did* say that to Dion.

Whatever the case, Dion Fortune found much that she disliked in the Golden Dawn and in 1927 formed the Fraternity of the Inner Light, which later became the Society of the Inner Light, which is still in operation today. Her main and most accurate legacy, however, is her books, all of which I heartily recommend. Dion Fortune is certainly a priestess to whose level the contemporary representative of the Goddess can but aspire.

The Priestess Path to Date

One more person deserves a mention in the revival of the arts of the priestess: Aleister Crowley. His female counterpart, or 'Scarlet Woman', was often considered to be essential to his magickal work, though the voltages he elicited in these women seem to have in many cases broken the vessel. He occasionally *became* the priestess, as when he took a vow of obedience to Leah Hirsig during a cocaine frenzy and became the priestess 'Alys', as described in his Magickal Record.

The Thelemic* priestesses certainly provide an interesting contrast to those of the Golden Dawn, who were predominantly extremely chaste despite their liberated ideas – indeed, Maud Gonne once said to William Yeats, 'I have a horror of physical love' (hardly surprising, as she had become pregnant by her married lover at an early age and much personal trauma had ensued). Crowley would not have found such an attitude much good for what he had in mind. His magickal work was extreme, as was the creativity of his priestesses, for as long as they survived it. His one-time wife Rose Kelly, for example, was pivotal to the delivery of *The Book of the Law*, now the 'bible' of Thelema,

Crowley's school of belief. Leila Waddell, another of his Scarlet Women, was a ninth degree of the initiate O.T.O.,* and clearly a more active priestess. Leah Hirsig, one of his mistresses, was also magickally powerful in her own right.

The woman plays the central role in the Thelemic Gnostic Mass, though the level of her empowerment is highly debatable. She represents the Goddess, certainly, and emanates the wavelengths necessary to the work in hand.

To bring us right up to date, Kenneth Grant* vaunts a more complex form of the art of the priestess, inspired by the Tantric Vama-Marg practices I mentioned earlier, involving the particular essences of the priestess, known as *Kalas*, being used to specific magickal ends. Here the priestess becomes a living laboratory of the Goddess, alchemically investing biological matter with particular wavelengths.

This overview has been necessarily brief. However, it is enough to inform us in a measured sense that the legacy we are left as modern priestesses, or potential ones, is an amalgam of ancient practices and very new ideas and influences.

Through the mediation of the groups and individuals I've just mentioned and others I haven't had time to, the word 'priestess' has been re-introduced into modern parlance.

Basic Techniques for Finding
Your Inner Priestess

Now let us get down to basics and see how you, as an ordinary-seeming woman or man, can access the many and various qualities we have just witnessed.

I wanted to highlight the specific achievements of priestesses past in order to evoke their archetypal energies and to inspire the modern priestess with perhaps the most important quality required for accessing the inner luminary – the fire of passion. There are many types of priestess, as we have just seen, but one thing unites them all: they are devoted to their causes. Whether these be political, humanitarian, artistic or directly spiritual, they all involve a specific intent. Clarity of intent is an essential factor in the life of any magickally active person – indeed, this may be applied to anyone. The means to manifest this intent are something we shall be looking at in this chapter.

MIND-BODY-SPIRIT: ALIGNING THE PHYSICAL SELF WITH TRUE WILL

I am not going to tell you what your intentions as a priestess ought to be, as they are different for each of us, and as we have already discussed, there are as many different types of priestess as there are types of woman. Chances are, if you have been drawn to this book, you already have some idea of what you wish to manifest in this life. These are personal aims. Success with creative pursuits, happiness, health and so on are wonderful springboards to help us on our way to higher ideals, but for the priestess they are not the end result. However, nearly all of us are compromised in the initial stages by the sheer difficulty of manifesting these primary situations, never mind advancing to world healing, working with Goddesses and other divine beings, and the other roles of the priestess.

First of all, we are going to look at practical ways to shake off the mundane. It is wonderful to read of priests and priestesses, mystics and yogis who have succeeded in their endeavours and to experience the effects of their work first-hand, but actually emulating their wavelengths may well be another matter. I have met quite a few people in my role as a psychic counsellor who have become despondent because some books make connection with the divine seem so easy that they feel like failures for not being able to astrally project, or achieve communion with spirits, or whatever their aim might be. In fact, it is perfectly normal to undergo at least stages of inability to connect – we are not all designed to be full-on space cadets! Most of us have to work for a living, most of us have bills to pay and others to care for, and in any case, absolutely all of us have hindrances which we would not consciously choose if we could help it. We certainly all have bodies and egos and their concomitant needs and programming and effects. So let's stop and be utterly down to earth for a moment and consider what you can do to get yourself into the condition required to access your inner priestess.

We will begin by looking at the body, which despite cliché really is your temple and certainly is the temple of the Goddess.

Practical head-dresses on now, please!

PREPARING THE BODY

It is common amongst the spiritually minded to neglect physical health. Sometimes the physical plane is considered too transient and superficial to merit attention, or the motivation is simply lacking. I know very few truly physically fit priestesses, for example – certainly few as fit as me and some of my friends. I do not wish to vaunt my efforts in any egocentric way, but am simply telling you what I know from my own direct experience. It's called effort, and anyone can do it, in whatever form. My personal *bhakti* to the Goddesses of the body is to run a minimum of four miles a day, and I feel the benefit on every level.

It is my belief and knowledge that mind, body and spirit are all essential elements of the working whole. I feel that women (particularly in the UK) ought to take a more proactive approach to physical well-being. Instead of focusing on external beauty, with make-up, fad diets and nip 'n' tucks, how much better to get our energy centres going via constructive exercise! This of course gives us greater leeway to occasionally indulge in the much-needed vices ...

Physical exercise brings many benefits to the priestess. Whether her preferred form is jogging, racing, swimming, sailing (like the modern sea priestess, Ellen McArthur), cycling or even working out at the gym, exercise facilitates a form of *pranayama* – that is, steady deep breathing which creates meditative states *(see page 51)*. Some of my own best ideas come to me while I'm running. Not only this, but exercise is a fantastic way to tune in to the elements – in the case of running, those of Earth and Air; in the case of swimming, those of Water and Air.

It is also hugely important to basic physical and spiritual health to receive at least half an hour of natural light daily, and preferably much more. Natural light (including Moon and starlight when available) is essential to the balance between the physical, etheric and spiritual bodies. On a basic level, it affects the brain and the amount of serotonin it produces. Sunlight is the most beneficial in this context.

If swimming in a pool or the sea is not your idea of fun, then it is possible to invest your bath or shower with ritual import. Just as baths are cleansing to the physical body, so they can cleanse and protect the etheric and spiritual bodies too.

One simple technique that I use daily involves holding a handful of sea salt to the East, asking the Goddess for cleansing and visualizing it being invested with vivid light (usually electric blue, sometimes orange, depending on whether I mainly require cleansing or strength). As the salt is dropped into the running water, the 'light' is seen spreading throughout the bath. When it is bright and lustral to the psychic eye, I get in.

Whilst relaxing and washing, you can envisage the day's strains and psychic pollutants dissolving from the body and into the bath, where they are either instantly dissolved or sent down the plughole as the water runs away.

Obviously this basic (yet truly ancient) structure of ritual cleansing and bathing may be enhanced and adapted for any situation. Gemstones, essential oils, incense and coloured candles of suitable correspondences will help focus your mind on a specific intent. For example, to enhance the atmosphere of love in your home or life, use scents and symbols sacred to Venus – rose, pink quartz, seashells, etc. Use your imagination, or failing that, some of the many excellent books available on the subject *(see Recommended Reading)*.

Dance is another wonderful way to contact your priestess-self on a basic level. Since you are seeking the most empowered and genuine version of yourself, and attuning it to your Higher Will, your music should be inspiring, your movements free-flowing and your thoughts uninhibited. Dancing bears a close relationship to shamanism and can facilitate higher or altered states of consciousness. It is a huge aide to visualization. Many priestesses experience synaesthesia* and are carried into visual and astral worlds by sound. The art of movement and dance is explored in depth in the wonderful works of Gabrielle Roth and Sharron Rose *(see Recommended Reading)*.

Diet is of course part of the mind-body-spirit dynamic. It goes without saying that foods which are *prana*-rich (such as fresh fruit and vegetables) are more spirit-enhancing than those which are not (dried and processed foods, packaged carbohydrates, etc). Priestesses of old used to facilitate trance states by altering their diets prior to ritual (and often fasting in advance also); some would eat only apples (the Druidic priestesses), others would be fed on nothing but honey (the priestesses of Apollo), others would take only ritual drinks such as peppermint and barley (the priestesses of Demeter and Persephone). I am not suggesting for a moment that you attempt to survive only on honey for a week, but the point is, aligning one's diet to one's intentions will cause it to magnetically attract the desired wavelength.

Other paths to the Goddess in everyday life include the therapeutic arts, such as painting, making music, yoga, meditation and so on. These aspects are too well explored to go into here, but are all activities which facilitate a state conducive to finding the inner priestess.

Let us look now at how all and any of the above basics may be conjoined with various other techniques in order to bring about the magickal state of mind required by the potential priestess.

SYMBOLIZING YOUR INTENT AS A PRIESTESS: PARAPHERNALIA AND THE ALTAR

Outward trappings and paraphernalia are not essential by any means, but they can be extremely helpful props, especially in the initial stages of your path as a priestess. Apart from anything else, physical objects act as subconscious prompts about the aims that originally went into their acquisition. This is why many witches make their own tools and decorate them with sigils and other marks of intent. You may like to do the same thing via a gemstone, piece of jewellery or even a body-marking such a tattoo. The point is to select something that represents your aspirations as a priestess, what you wish to attain. You focus on this while you meditate and ask for aid in becoming the luminary you wish to be, and it is thus invested with all of your Goddess-felt energy.

I know many who have selected a moonstone to fulfil this role; it is certainly a stone of huge relevance to the priestess, representing Magick, lunar and intuitive energy and the liminal worlds. However, it is important that you select the right thing for yourself. You then carry or wear it in all of the situations in which your magickal belief is challenged or drained. With the object as your portable priestess symbol, you will soon become accustomed to carrying this persona into everyday life with you.

Another touchstone for the priestess is of course the altar. I strongly recommend that each and every priestess, potential or otherwise, builds herself an altar to act as an interface between herself and the deities and spirits. The altar should be placed somewhere where it will not be disturbed and in a position which intuitively feels positive. It is usual to place the altar in the East side of the space, in the quarter in which the Sun rises. Obviously this represents the principles of illumi-nation and redemption.

The altar, which soon develops a spiritually organic energy of its own, provides the perfect platform on which to place one's votive offerings such as flowers and foodstuffs, photos of people or places to be healed, precious magickal objects and, if you like, statues of your deities. Magickal working tools may also be kept here, such as the chalice, athame (a ritual dagger used to direct energy, to cut unwanted ties and for lateral functions) and the wand (an energy-conducting stick, basically).

The altar provides the place of magickal focus for the priestess. It gives us a psychic continuum with which to work. It does not have to be a complex or costly affair; indeed, a simple fold-out table or fold-out altar will do (the latter are available in many forms, especially in Eastern countries; I suspect they are also on sale over the internet). These are ideal for those who do not have the space or the privacy to keep an altar standing at all times.

The altar space may be kept clean by flicking salt-water over it and visualizing it as a place glowing with white-blue light. Make sure that dying flowers and other symbols of decline are removed from the altar on a regular basis.

The altar space will act as a sort of allegory to the inner eye of one's own spiritual progress. If it does not look 'bright' and progressive to your inner eye, invite the Goddess to bless it. Isis is a particularly apt deity to call on for this, for she represents both Magick and growth on all levels. The Indian Goddess Laxmi will bring the golden light of beneficence and good luck with her when she graces your altar with her divine presence. These Goddesses and many others are detailed later in this book (Chapter 6).

Keep your altar dynamic and enjoy its many moods. Whenever possible, conduct your inner workings and magickal rituals in its proximity, bearing in mind that almost all human endeavour is magickally significant in some sense, even if not the obvious. For example, as I write this I am sitting opposite my altar, on which I have three votive candles burning. Also on the altar – which is silver and copper, incidentally – are a silver chalice filled with red wine for the Goddess and spirits and a lemon puff. (The spirits love lemon puffs, I am not quite sure why. Go to any Eastern temple and you will see the altar stacked high with them. Other offerings include fresh fruit, condensed milk and incense.) To the right of my altar is a statue of Horus, son of Isis, with whom I have been working lately. A pentacle made by a close friend also rests on the altar, beneath which a heap of spells is fermenting and various oils and gemstones are charging. The point is that the altar is being used to help me focus magickal energies of futurity, even though I am not directly working Magick right now.

As you too will find out, if you haven't already, the altar serves as a stage on which your inner priestess will make much progress and as a gateway to different levels of consciousness.

PROTECTING YOURSELF

Many magickally-minded people's worst enemy is themselves, so this section should probably be entitled 'Protecting yourself from yourself'! It is part of the nature of the priestess to be highly sensitive – indeed, this is an actual requirement. The repercussions of this quality include taking things to heart, perhaps becoming pessimistic or disenchanted with the world and its nightmares, suffering vicariously by absorbing the feelings of others and similar inconveniences. Therefore protection is vital for any priestess.

Psychic Self-Protection Techniques

There are many well-known psychic protection and grounding techniques, such as the Qabalistic Cross and the invocation of the Archangels Raphael, Michael, Gabriel and Uriel. A salt bath vivified by creative visualization *(see below)* also works wonders.

In my opinion, the technique that works best, simple though it is, is to ask for help from your patron deity or Angel, or your guide(s) on the inner planes, if you are aware of them. Light a candle and some incense and offer it to the entity concerned. Envisage them surrounding you with a symbol of protection, such as a circle of fire that fends off the wild animals of the universe – that is, negative or encroaching energies. Usually the imagery will happen spontaneously.

There are also traditional folk methods of defending your home and self from psychic attack or general maleficence, such as the making of a 'Witch's Bottle', a glass bottle (usually green) into which sharp objects such as nails are placed, along with broken glass, pins, urine (of the woman of the house) and thread (usually red). It is then buried in the garden, hidden under the floorboards or kept by the door or a window.

There are many other Witchcraft-based objects and amulets for self-protection, some of which are detailed in Nathaniel J. Harris's book *Witcha: A Book of Cunning (see Recommended Reading).*

WILL POWER: HOW TO BRING ABOUT MAGICKAL MANIFESTATIONS

Creative Visualization

Creative visualization is such a powerful magickal technique that its implications are quite terrifying! The magickal adage 'Be careful what you wish for' is very true and should perhaps be followed by 'And beware what you imagine!' Every thought, every image, creates a possibility, an expectation. We are most likely to fulfil the images we project the most, provided we make moves on the Earth plane to bring them to pass. The call of the day is thus to think and visualize positively. Of course, this is often not easy and sometimes cures for emotional trauma and past-life issues are required to liberate one from difficult challenges. *(See the section on healing, page 117.)*

People's habitual thoughts are written all over their faces and bodies. This is particularly evident when one begins to age – usually in the mid-thirties, though this can be much earlier or later, depending on many factors. Stress, depression and optimism are some of the major influences. The optimistic person or calmly positive person will often seem a great deal younger than the person who has undergone periods of stress and depression and has experienced hopelessness. The 'give up and die' attitude is the first step towards ageing yourself dramatically on all levels.

I have learned through experience that when faced with this conundrum the best way out is to *ask* for help from the deities and many helpful spirits who wish to aid humanity's progress and then to make active moves to help yourself.

Setting a goal is one way to create light at the end of the tunnel. Long-term plans enthusiastically pursued will rejuvenate the body as well as the spirit. Aspiration affects matter through its upbeat vibration and can bring about instant rejuvenation.

Most powerfully of all, our thoughts directly affect our bodies. This is not exactly groundbreaking news of course and has been elaborately explored in many books of popular psychology and New Age metaphysics. The works of Gill Edwards, Deepak Chopra and Shakti Gawain are recommended if you are unfamiliar with the basics *(see Recommended Reading)*. With this as a conscious factor, however, it is possible to think yourself youthful and beautiful and, more importantly for the priestess, powerful (in conjunction with actual effort, of course). It is also possible to dramatically slow the physical and psychological ageing process (that is, disenchantment) by visualizing your future self as glamorous, healthy and still progressing magickally. The Crone is without doubt a most wonderful face of the Goddess, indicating wisdom and experience, but few of us wish to reflect this aspect in our physical beings before we really need to. Maud Gonne looked drop-dead gorgeous and utterly captivating well into her seventies and eighties. Why? Because she embodied the Goddess in *all* of her aspects, including Maiden and Mother, even when she was physically a Crone. She used this to enhance her work as a priestess. We can all do this. It's called agenda, and it provokes charisma.

Now that many of us live well into our seventies, and some reach much more advanced ages, we have positive role-models to encourage us. Instead of cowering inside our bodies and waiting for death (or Godot), we can use this powerful time to really explore ourselves as spiritual beings. I believe that one of the reasons why spirituality has 'returned' to the West in recent years is that some older people have used their 'time out' to re-evoke the paths of the Ancients. Indeed, as somebody who attends conferences on Witchcraft and the like, I know this to be true.

The consciousness of our elders is actively restimulating our respect for and knowledge of the spiritual realms. This is because these many and various characters, now devoid of the craving for status and power which affects us younger people, have agreed to be 'stripped of their beauty', their outward trappings, and to stand up and offer themselves as guides. Our elders, or some of them, are like low-level bodhisattvas, compassionate spirits who have agreed not to ascend until 'the last human is saved'. Obviously this is too tall an order for most of our elders, but some, I feel sure, have outlived their natural years for a specific purpose, albeit not quite as lofty a one as that of the bodhisattvas. Still, they can teach us, either through their books or through their words when we interact with them.

There are some pretty amazing older people, particularly women, out there on the contemporary magickal scene. How wonderful to meet open-minded individuals who have also 'been there and done that'. I might point out too that many of these people, though altered and marked by time, are still strikingly physically attractive, at least for their years, and often remarkably active.

I know one 75-year-old woman, Alice, who recently constructed a stone circle in her own back garden. She asked me to come over and take a look at it, which I duly did, and then she mentioned that one of the stones looked a little too far to the right. She asked me to shift it; I am embarrassed to say that I was unable to help out on that one. The old lady, who is a witch and High Priestess, sighed, walked over, lifted the rock clean out of the ground and replaced it where she had decided it ought to be. So much for the strength and vigour of youth and the frailty of age!

Youth culture as perpetuated by the media has a very great deal to answer for in terms of loss of empathy between generations. In ancient times, our elders would have been revered and their insight used to advantage. However, Western aesthetic ideals have destroyed this dynamic. I strongly suspect that the heart of the pop-culture industry would not weigh lightly against the feather of Maat.

It used to be the case in Western society that the few old people around were riddled with disease and discomfort. This was still true only a hundred or so years ago. So our image of 'age' was negative in the extreme. People approached the process of getting older with a sense of dread and horror, and the negative image became a self-fulfilling prophecy. Now, thanks to the spread of medicine and health care, and to positive attitudes to retirement now prevalent in the West, we can now look forward to long and prosperous years of sunshine rather than twilight. Because of this positive image of ageing, more and more of us are experiencing long and fulfilling life-spans. This gives us more time to work as active priests and priestesses. Our creative visualizations no longer carry wholly negative messages about physical progression. The same principle can be applied to any aspect of life.

As a basic grounding, any worker with Spirit has to look at their psychological blueprints and influence them in the most positive manner possible. This is one of the first lessons in magickal training. Counsellors are required to undergo counselling as part of their training. Reiki practitioners undergo Reiki as part of theirs. The priestess is rarely born whole. If she were, then her compassion might be limited, and compassion is one of the most essential assets of the priestess. It later becomes empathy, but it is never sympathy, as this implies pity. The priestess does not pity others, except on a grand scale, and that includes herself. On an individual level, she at least begins her incarnation in as vulnerable a way as everyone else and as such she is willing to approach her own weaknesses and work with (rather than against) them. All of our issues and vulnerabilities are here for a reason.

So, let us look at some of the possible effects of creative visualization and self-reprogramming, or deprogramming.

One anecdotal example: I had a friend, Anne, who was terrified of horses. Bizarrely, her father's father had been trampled to death by a herd of wild horses in Canada before she was born. Her father had raised her to believe that horse-riding was dangerous, that she might be thrown at a fence and break her back, that the horse might buck at any moment, and so on. As a consequence of this mental and psychological training, my friend found herself terrified of horses and later in life she went through a stage of agoraphobia, which I strongly suspect was connected to the horse issue (fear of open spaces and vulnerability to attack being key factors). The negative images had been programmed into her mind so effectively that even a picture of a horse, or the thought of one, would chemically affect her, so that she got an adrenalin rush and felt panicky. Many who suffer from vertigo will experience the same effect looking at a picture of a high view or thinking about standing on a rooftop, etc. Many phobias elicit the same or similar effects. Our bodies are hugely affected by our responses, both those that are natural to us and those that are programmed.

If Anne had been taught as a child that horses were magickal creatures who had long been friends to humanity and that we could move with speed and grace and pleasure over long distances on their backs, free as the wind, she would most likely have become a passionate and competent rider. Psychically and psychologically speaking, she needed to be rewired in order to even begin to overcome her blocks. We all have our own equivalents, whether they manifest as obvious phobias such as this, or simply as self-doubt, self-sabotage and panic over our own capabilities.

None of us can help the messages that are programmed into us during childhood. But all parents should be aware of their own reactions and the subsequent implications for their susceptible children.

Thankfully, whatever our own programming, we are able to create new images and messages and to reprogramme ourselves. One of the many wonderful things about the human condition is that we have a huge capacity for recovery. So even if you have been through terrible experiences (which many of us have, for one reason or another), it is essential to learn from but not to dwell on them. Being angry, embittered or 'injured' is death to the magickal life. Process, forgive, learn and let go. This is a key stage of recovery – and you owe it to yourself to recover. Life is fluid and can become anything we visualize it to be. So think magickally!

Here is one of many possible ways to do this.

 ## Creatively Visualizing Yourself in the Future

The importance of a positive self-image cannot be overemphasized. On a daily basis, be sure to visualize yourself as strong, wise, healthy, beautiful and powerful, including at the age of 70 – and watch your image fulfil itself!

- *Perform one of the pranayama techniques (see pages 51–53) or simply take a few slow, deep, cleansing breaths.*

- *When you are breathing calmly and deeply, strongly visualize yourself in the future – preferably about five years ahead or more – looking and being just the way you wish to be, surrounded by the things you most wish to acquire. Be sure to make your image powerful and positive.*

- *Now imagine a ball of yellow light between your eyebrows. Send it out to meet the same area on the head of your future self, so that you are joined by a bridge of light at your respective third eyes.*

- *Transfer your consciousness into this future self. Notice how shapely your body is, how strong, and how wise and happy your future self is, surrounded by all that has been achieved so far - compositions completed, books written, artwork perfected, doctorates gained and so on, as is appropriate to your aspirations.*

- *Think of all the things you did to become this way - your ongoing aims, the efforts taken to remain magickal, fit and healthy.*

- *Have an inner dialogue with your selves at this point, if you desire.*

- *Still in the consciousness of your future body, look at your younger self and tap them on the forehead. 'Deliver' the solidity of this real future self into your present consciousness and keep the lines of light bright and definite.*

- *Now return your consciousness back to your present self by sending the ball of light back down the line into your third eye area.*

- *There is no need to get rid of the line which connects you.*

- *Return to your daily consciousness and keep this picture in your mind. Use it as an impetus to help you exercise, work towards your goals and to think optimistically about your long-term future. It's an investment in the Etheric Bank. You are creating the profit in both spellings right now.*

Through techniques such as the one just described it is possible to clear some of the debris out of one's life and think positively in a psychological and spiritual manner.

What, however, about the magickal wavelengths that any priestess requires to be present in her life?

First, we will need the persona to deal with and direct these energies. So far, the inner priestess may simply be an idea, an aspiration or a part of the personality that only comes through once in a while.

Here is one way to connect with the inner priestess on a more regular, if not permanent basis. I have used the Goddess Isis in this exercise, but obviously you can use any deity with whom you feel a rapport and whom you feel you might like to serve as a priestess.

 ## Inviting your Inner Priestess to Come Forth

Try to get into a magickal mood. This may involve listening to music that you find particularly inspiring, meditating or praying, having a ritual bath with candles and incense, or walking somewhere of import such as a cemetery or by a body of water.

- Light three candles of whatever colour appeals to you most at the time. Try to pick a colour that either enhances your sense of self or symbolizes something that is missing in your life. If you could absorb any colour into yourself right now, what would it be? Pick that one.

- Light the candles and place them on your altar or in a place which is positive to you.

- Light a joss-stick or some loose incense and hold it to the East. As you do so, imagine Isis (or your chosen deity) standing there, so that she is actually in the room with you, just a little behind the veil of realities. Offer the incense to her and then draw a wide circle around yourself using the smoke to delineate its boundaries. As you circum-navigate the space you are in, be aware of the Goddess appearing at each of the cardinal points – East, South, West and then North – and finally surrounding you entirely.

- Face the candles and focus on their flames, which are visible not just in this dimension, but in several others too.

- Envisage Isis standing behind your altar. Also, ask her to come and bless you. Isis never refuses a request for aid.

- As you evoke her, through word or simply through concentration, stand before the altar with your legs slightly parted and your arms in a 'Y' gesture in order to best capture her energies.

- She wears a crescent Moon on her forehead and her clothes are as white as moonshine on water. In her right hand she carries an Ankh, the Egyptian symbol of health, the union of opposites and immortality.

- As the Goddess of both Magick and speech, you may find that Isis has something to say to you which is entirely personal and cannot be predicted here. This is more than likely.

- Commune with her. Tell her that you wish to find your inner priestess and to become the most competent representative of the divine, particularly the feminine divine, that you can manage. Ask her to bless you and guide you along the path.

- Then focus on yourself as a miniature version of the Goddess, with your unique array of experiences, qualities and abilities. Imagine these conjoining with the image and the qualities of Isis.

- Now meditate on yourself as a priestess of Isis and explore the theme, either visually or intuitively (we all work in different ways with this kind of thing). You may like to make notes or sketches about what you perceive, as often these things are swiftly forgotten as soon as ordinary consciousness is regained.

- When you feel you have gained all that you can for the present, thank Isis (or the Goddess you have been working with) and record your experience. This will help to solidify it in your mind and over time you will build up a valuable record of your experiences and progress.

PRANAYAMA

Pranayama – yogic breath control – is a way of refining the senses by focusing on mind, body and spirit. It stimulates temporal lobe activity, as do all effective forms of meditation, yoga and religious or magickal contemplation. Pranayama also facilitates the absorption of life-sustaining energy from light, air and the essence of the cosmos. 'Breath', meaning 'life', is particularly sacred to the Goddess Isis, patroness of arts magickal and thus of priestesses of any tradition.

There are three simple breathing methods for gathering prana from the atmosphere:

1   The first is holding the breath in before exhaling it and then pausing before inhaling again.

2   The second is doing this to the full capacity of your lungs. Most of us only use a tiny fraction of our lung capacity except, ironically, whilst smoking. This is one of the reasons why smokers find cigarettes relaxing – it is the only time they inhale, retain the breath and exhale in a relaxed and yogic manner! Indeed, a great aid to giving up the habit is to simply imagine you are smoking and do the breathing as if you were.

3   The third simple pranic technique is to visualize the prana entering your lungs and spreading into your system as brilliant gold-yellow light or whichever colour is appropriate to you at the time. This kind of breathing can be used to absorb energy for healing, self-revitalization and all sorts of magickal work.

Another easy form of *pranayama* is to breathe in deeply through the nose, hold the breath for a comfortable moment – usually around 5–7 seconds – and then breathe out through the mouth whilst visualizing golden atoms flowing in as you inhale and silvery-white ones exiting your body.

It is incredible how quickly this process becomes effective – especially with practice. It will not be long before you feel fully recharged and, importantly, become attuned to the psycho-magickal changes in your body. Working with this and the other techniques described in this book, you stand a very good chance of developing second sight or of enhancing the psychic abilities you already have. They will also increase your magickal intent, or Will.

You may also like to try the following technique.

Pranayama *Technique for 'Positive' Breathing*

This technique is particularly good for those of us who live in built-up areas and do not receive enough truly fresh air. As one who lives and runs in London, I use this *pranayama* visualization frequently. It helps to keep me sane and counteracts urban claustrophobia.

● *Visualize a natural place full of fresh air, preferably somewhere you love. I use the snow-peaked Himalayan mountains or the Cornish coastline, depending on my mood.*

● *Breathe in, strongly visualizing the air coming at you across space and Time from your chosen location.*

● *Hold it for a moment, then breathe it back out, being sure to 'return' it to the same location.*

● *Carry on for as long as you wish.*

In performing this simple exercise, you achieve three things. One, you create a trans-dimensional link with that place and receive the air astrally, etherically and spiritually – which means in most of your bodies. Secondly, you creatively visualize and 'experience' in a way that will affect your brain. Your brain will believe that you really are in the location of your choice (even though you consciously refute it) and your body will respond accordingly. Thirdly, you will steady your breathing and create a positive wavelength in your mind and bodies.

This technique can also be used during rhythmic exercise to great effect.

LIGHT, COLOUR AND APPROACHING CELESTIAL HELPERS

Light-breathing is another useful breathing exercise. It involves meditating on rays of a certain colour and absorbing them into your bodies for cleansing, healing and lateral purposes. The colour is 'inhaled' and perceived by the inner eye to be infusing first the lungs and then the entire body, particularly any parts that might require specific physical or spiritual healing. Often the light takes on a life of its own, moving naturally to the affected areas and highlighting issues of which one might not have been consciously aware. This process can be enhanced through the use of coloured light bulbs or light filters, but this is not essential. Outdoors is definitely the best venue. Of course you can improvise as necessary or simply use meditation and breathing.

I often do my light-breathing when I run. As one who works in central London and often socializes in places filled with cigarette smoke (and who has herself been known to smoke after a glass of wine or two!), it is important to me to 'give something back' to my lungs.

After a couple of miles of steady fast running, I start to visualize myself surrounded by white light, though sometimes it occurs naturally as purple or green, depending on what my bodies require at the time. I deeply and consciously inhale this light while I hold a sort of inner dialogue with my lungs, encouraging them to give me the particles that they no longer want to hold. I imagine each alveolus expelling whatever matter is unhelpful or detrimental to it and thank the whole organs for allowing me to run like the wind despite their compromise.

The heart is also affected by pollution and usually the white light begins to infuse that too within moments.

As I continue to run, the colours shift and change dramatically. As I inhale, I visualize the purifying, rejuvenating white light entering my lungs. I think of their strength and their capacity (we use only a fraction of our lungs most of the time. Physical exercise and, ironically, smoking, are two of the few chances they get to expand). As I exhale, with a big puff, I see the particles of debris and pollution exiting my lungs. Very often this is physically visible, like exhaling cigarette smoke, and I don't just mean on cold days! It often happens on warm or even hot days, and as the exhaled psychic and physical matter is not always white or grey smoke, but sometimes other colours, I think that we can safely assume that it's more than just condensation!

This is an example of physical and auric healing, but the same process may be carried out for many other purposes. Heightening the pace of the body and the flow of the blood also increases levels of *prana*, essential life-energy, and speeds up all life-enhancing processes. As you run, swim, bathe, work out or simply perform *pranayama*, inhale the coloured light that you most need. See it all around you. It will soon develop in your perceptions and you will feel the benefit on many levels.

Each colour has its own properties and various deities whose wavelength is the same. You might like to ask one of these deities to help bring you the colour and healing that you need. In the table below, you'll find some comments on each colour, including its use, some ways to access it and some of the deities or celestial helpers concomitant to that wavelength.

BASIC LIGHT–COLOUR CORRESPONDENCES

Rose	Emotional Healing, Love, Comfort, Relaxation
	Isis, Aphrodite, Kuan-Yin
	Excellent colour to work with in the bath, or for comforting and healing others, especially children and those unaccustomed to the practices of the priestess. Rose quartz is a very effective epitome of the powers of this colour.
Emerald Green	Physical rejuvenation, Cleanliness, Joy and Love, Heart issues
	Osiris, Freya, Brigit/Bride, Isis, Gaea, Pan, Dionysus
	If you can afford it, an emerald will benefit health and growth greatly. Green is rarely seen in the aura as a whole, except in those crossing from childhood into spiritual adulthood, but it may be observed in or directed to specific organs. Encourages proliferation.
Electric Blue	Magick, Karma, Pure Power, Cleanliness, Protection
	Artemis, Athena, Krishna, Siva
	Fabulous for use in general Magick (the colour with which most items are charged), psychism, telepathy, and self-protection. Usually accessed through ritual acts and visualization. Also connected to lustral workings, particularly with sea salt. If you live in a sunless clime, you can access this wavelength via a solarium or UV lamp. Be sure to visualize the Moon or Sun (as apt) as you soak in a few rays.
Red	Self-protection against attack, Energy
	Kali, Durga, Anubis, Seth
	Breathing and meditating on red stimulates the base chakra, but also develops bravery and the will to

	fight for just causes. Objects made of iron increase its power.
White or Silvery White	Spiritual protection, Blessing, Detoxification, both physical and emotional, Eloquence
	Isis, Selene, Thoth, Mercury, Sarasvati
	The all-purpose colour, it brings instant blessings and lessening of karma however it is accessed.
Gold, Yellow	Prosperity, Health, Spiritual blessing, Intellect, Health
	Demeter, Hathor, Laxmi, Horus, the bodhisattvas, Apollo
	Excellent beneficent colour to visualize and breathe. Seen in auras of others it denotes compassion, intellect, mysticism and East-meets-West, spiritually speaking. Easily accessed in direct sunlight, particularly at sunrise or sunset.
Purple	Magick, Reverence, Spirituality, Dignity, Re-attunement, Dreams, Esoteric Lore
	Persephone, Hera, Nephthys, Thoth
	Can be worn and breathed to great effect. Purple auras usually denote those with strong sense of ego-self, spiritual interests and great charismatic power.
Black	Self-protection, Renewal, Rebirth, Power, both physical and psychological
	Hecate, Khephri, the Cailleach, Nuit, Kali
	Best worn or used as astral concealing cloak. Black auras in others are often temporary fall-out of bad moods and temper. 'Evil' people are usually much too clever to wear black in their auras.

MANTRAS

There is a strong connection between sound as a formula and life. In Hinduism this principle is represented by Brahma, who created the world through his speech. Similarly, in Egyptian myth Thoth created the Ogdoad, the elements, from the sound vibration of words.

Words and sounds create and sustain and can also destroy. Experiments have been performed to create a sound that can kill – and there certainly are such wavelengths. Obviously, we will be focusing here on those that cause positive change and those that create. Sound can be used to attract a desired object or set of circumstances, to shift obstacles (to a surprisingly literal degree) and to create a receptive and positive wavelength in the practitioner. The most effective form of this is the use of seed-sounds such as 'AUM' and then a mantra.

Mantras operate in a creative and sustaining manner to enliven specific bodily responses and affect the astral, etheric and spiritual bodies. The more they are repeated, both internally and externally, the more powerful they become. They are rather like prayers in that they often involve supplication and worship of a particular deity or representative of certain qualities and energies, but they are also self-empowering and actually change one's physical, astral and spiritual constitution as they are recited.

Most mantras commonly used today are Hindu, so we will discuss these briefly first. *(See the Recommended Reading for further ideas if the use of Hindu mantras holds especial appeal for you.)*

Certain mantras are particularly good at generating 'cosmic food' or divine sustenance. This creates a feeling of being nurtured on all levels and brings divine solicitude. One such is the Krishna mantra *Hare Krishna, Hare Krishna, Krishna Krishna, Hare Hare, Hare Rama, Hare Rama, Rama Rama, Hare Hare.*

Krishna is intimately connected with the idea of divine beneficence and many tales of his youth involve him stealing milk, drinking milk and laterally being blessed by the Great Mother. Through Krishna, we perceive the Divine Mother as a protective and nurturing source of creation. Followers of Krishna the globe over cook food and bless it before distributing it amongst the needy. This wonderful act of humanity reflects the concept of being provided for on every level in a blessed cosmos. To those with psychic vision, the food so blessed literally glows with *prana*.

Other mantras suited to the purpose of self-sustenance and increased power include those of Laxmi and Siva. Incidentally, most (though not all) mantras end in *Namaha* if one is under 28 and in *Swaha* if one is older.

Laxmi is a Goddess of health, wealth and well-being, thus echoes the concept of being surrounded by goodness in the universe. Even the air in which Laxmi's ghee-lamps shine will sustain the devotee.

Laxmi's mantra is as follows: *Om Shrim Maha Lakshmiyei Namaha* (if you are under 28), and *Om Shrim Maha Lakshmiyei Swaha* (if you are over 28). Chanting this mantra will bring extra energy, optimism and creativity as well as health and increased prosperity.

About five years ago, a member of my family who had no prior experience of working with Hindu deities decided to use the Laxmi mantra and a visualization of her I had written for my book *Invoke the Goddess (see Recommended Reading)* shortly before an important job interview. Rather sceptically at first, he followed the visualization and allowed Laxmi to appear in his inner vision, unfurling from a lotus flower and shining her glorious golden light into his life. Before long, as he told me excitedly afterwards, the vision had taken on a whole new life of its own and he was actively communing with the Goddess. Filled with optimism and enthusiasm, he went off to the job interview. He still holds the post today.

Siva, on the other hand, is a God of asceticism and destruction, who lives in solitude in his Himalayan retreat, subsisting off yoga and hashish. His disciplined, fierce attitude cuts away at the temptation towards luxury and non-progressive indulgence of the senses and thus is of benefit to anyone in the process of self-refinement of any kind.

Siva's mantra is *Om Nama Shivaya*.

Siva's consort, when he has one, is Parvati, who also manifests as the Goddess Kali, whom we will be looking at in greater depth later in this book (Chapter 6). Her mantra is usually used to negate fear of Time and death – in other words, to remove the obstacles caused by the ego and by one's programming.

Parvati's mantra is *Om Krim Kaliklayei Namaha*.

Another rather fierce Goddess we will be looking at later is Durga. Though she appears at first sight to be delicate and gentle, a second glance reveals that she rides a lion or tiger and carries deadly weapons, all of which she is adept at using, and she spends more time on the cosmic battleground than off it! Durga was created by the male Gods to defeat a particularly obdurate demon, Mahisha. Thus she represents defence from evil and strength in adversity.

The mantra to chant for Durga's protection is *Om Dum Durgayei Namaha*. (For Durga, *Namaha* is used whatever one's age.)

Ganesh (or Ganesha) is the Hindu remover of obstacles and the God of physicians, good health and business. If you are being blocked by material circumstances, or a particular person, or by negative habits, Ganesha's mantra is ideal to complement your other practices. Focus on removing the obstacles that stand between you and an ideal situation while you chant *Om Gang Ganapatye Namaha*.

Other mantras which will help infuse you with a sense of youth, health and vigour include the following:

Om Sri Dhanvantre Namaha, *meaning 'Hail to the being and power of the Celestial Physician'. In traditional Hindu households, particularly in the south of India, this mantra is chanted over food as it is being prepared in order to maximize its positive properties and keep disease at bay. It can also be used to heal specific ailments. It should be repeated 12,500 times whilst focusing on the ailment to hand.*

Om Arkaya Namaha, *meaning 'Salutations to the Shining One who removes afflictions', is essentially a mantra to the Sun and thus makes a perfect accompaniment to channelling light into your food and bodies.*

For the priestess, a primary function is spiritual eloquence. If ideas and explanations are being blocked by lack of articulation, or if extra inspiration is required in the sacred arts (including those of literature, dance and music), then Saraswati is the Goddess on whom to call and whose mantra to employ. This beautiful Goddess of culture, speech and intellect may be meditated on through the mantra Om Eim Saraswatyei Swaha.

The mantra of the Goddess in her entirety, representing the creative force itself, is Om Shrim Shriyei Swaha, *which translates as 'Greetings to the feminine force of the Universe'.*

It is possible to create mantras which are Western in nature. In Transcendental Meditation, it is common to create a personal mantra for internal repetition during meditation. The idea is to focus on absolutely nothing other than this phrase. The main point of a mantra is the repetition of intent, although the tones in which it is repeated are also important. As already mentioned, it is the sound vibration within the words which carries them from the personal consciousness into the Cosmos.

The reader is encouraged to experiment and see what works best in different circumstances.

The Priestess as Seer and Oracle

A major role of the female within the mystery religions has always included that of Seeress. The art of divination is perhaps the most popular of magickal faculties; the ability to look into the future and predict the rise and fall of monarchs, the battle plans of enemy armies, the birth of heirs – in other words, the favours of the Gods – is worth a priestess's weight in gold.

Of course, the word of the oracle was not always heeded and Greek mythology and history tell of several scenarios which ended in disaster because predictions were ignored. One such tragic priestess was Cassandra, who according to Greek legend was so beautiful that Apollo fell in love with her. He agreed to give her the gift of prophecy if she would allow him to ravish her. She agreed, but once the gift was given, she backed out of her physical obligations. As punishment for her duplicity and out of pique for the scorn she had shown him, Apollo ruled that she should tell the truth in all her predictions, but that none should believe her. Thus Cassandra was perceived as a raving madwoman by her compatriots and despite her ability to foretell the fall of her native Troy, her dire predictions all came to pass.

Cassandra's tragedy illustrates that an accurate message may be delivered, but sometimes fate cannot be averted. Similarly, the clues and symbols may be given but it is up to the recipient to interpret them correctly. Shakespeare's witches in *Macbeth* invoke spirits whose messages are classically ambivalent: 'Be bloody, bold, and resolute; laugh to scorn/The power of man, for none of woman born/Shall harm Macbeth' and: 'Macbeth shall never vanquish'd be until/Great Birnam wood to high Dunsinane hill/Shall come against him.' Macbeth fails to decipher the oracle's terminology correctly, forgetting that MacDuff, who eventually kills him, was born by Caesarean section and was thus not 'of woman born', and failing to envisage the trees of Birnam wood being used as camouflage and shields by the enemy army. Because of these oversights, the accurate predictions he receives are worth nothing.

I used to work as a part-time Tarot reader and clairvoyant in an esoteric bookshop in central London. It always amused me to note that on the bottom of the official receipts was the phrase: 'N.B. It is the client's responsibility to interpret the reading.' Naturally the role of the reader is to explain as much as possible about the actual meanings of the cards, symbols and the psychic impressions received, but it is certain that ambivalence and misinterpretation are best avoided if the client becomes part of a two-way energy exchange. They know their own situation and inner symbology far better than anybody else possibly could, however psychically attuned that person may be, and by working with the reader they help facilitate an accurate and helpful reading. Sadly, some clients see the experience as a 'test' of one's psychic abilities and refuse to co-operate or, as they would see it, 'give anything away', thus stunting the power of the prediction and limiting the amount that may be fluently interpreted in the short time available, usually half an hour or an hour.

I mention this because predictions are sometimes oblique, or appear in symbol form, as demonstrated by the quotes above. This applies equally to psychic impressions regarding health, spirit contacts, past lives and a plethora of other areas. Sometimes it requires the recipient to help deduce why, for example, the image of a red rose entwined with a lily is appearing in their aura, or who the tall man standing behind them might be. At other times, a 'cold reading' may be accurately given (I did a great many of these due to the vast number of clients who do not wish to tell!), but without doubt interaction between reader and subject is highly desirable.

For the professional reader, the art of divination is necessarily couched in wordcraft. One must be articulate, swift and precise, and target the subject's level of linguistic comprehension, not to mention esoteric savvy. One client may barely be able to understand English (always a toughie, that one), requiring monosyllabic explanations and a greater degree of body language, together with telepathy where possible. The next might be an expert in semantics with years of occult study behind them. The effective oracle might well find their mercurial skills augmenting in response.

Such arts of articulation have not always been required of the priestess as Seer, however. In Ancient Egypt the priestesses of Thoth would simply bark like baboons and it was down to the priests to interpret the timbre and sense of their expostulations in a manner that might almost be described as synaesthetic. Here, the priestess or oracle acted purely as a channel, with no cerebral interpretation; this was a chthonic form of the art of divination (indeed, the 'Apes of Thoth' often worked in underground caves). The Pythias of Apollo played a similar role, stoned on laurel fumes and the miasmas which seeped from the underground fissures at Delphi. Fed almost entirely on honey and milk, these most famous of oracles surely had a few physical issues to deal with too, such as vitamin and mineral deficiencies and possible obesity, plus an almost permanent sugar-high. Some of Apollo's emissaries were highly eloquent, however, such as the aforementioned Cassandra.

In my years looking into this and lateral areas, I have noticed that there are physical resemblances between the people attracted to various spiritual techniques and beliefs. It makes sense that those of a particular genetic lineage might have a particular proclivity or skill, just like the Tribes of Israel, or the 'Atmans' (spiritual groups) of Hinduism.

It is worthy of note that many modern female 'mediums' and clairvoyants of the Doris Stokes/Spiritualist Church/School of Psychic Studies variety are large of girth, while the men tend to veer towards the slender or thin. A certain physique is attributable to those trained in a particular form of interaction with 'spirits of the dead', often via the mediation of 'spirit guides'. The women seem to require large amounts of sugar and carbohydrate to facilitate their work with 'Spirit', while the men seem to be more ascetic and work on their nerves.

Those involved with Paganism, Witchcraft, elemental work, angelic work and High Magick also show a general physical resemblance within each group – one that cuts deeper than sartorial self-expression, that is. It would not surprise me in the least if genetic links were discovered between those of particular paths, even when they are chosen rather than cultural. We all have different ways of accessing the Divine Intelligence.

Thus, the Seer will most likely be attracted to a particular mode of operation from the start. She may find that she is trained in one method for cultural or environmental reasons, but later deflects to a technique with which she is more comfortable. The means are not the point; the result is. However, it is interesting to look at some of the many methods available to the priestess as visionary.

Many people claim to be 'psychic', 'mediums', and so on. A cursory glance at the advertisements in even the most respectable of magazines and newspapers will reveal a startling demand for prediction, affirmation and advice of a non-empirical nature. It is interesting that in the UK, where belief in God is only held by around 55 per cent of the populace (according to MORI and other polls), belief in the occult is disproportionately high.

Many people either dismiss the art of prediction as balderdash or are terrified of it. Many have had bad experiences with moody or inaccurate mediums, astrologers and clairvoyants. As both recipient and giver of psychic impressions, it is important to keep your feet on the ground. I have worked in many situations with people who claim to be psychic and even those who are genuine can have a personally bad day, a psychically unattuned day or a block in their communication skills, which might lead their client to misinterpret their meaning. I spent two months working in an office with 12 other Tarot readers, for example, each of us on the end of a phone line. We worked from 8 in the evening until 4 in the morning taking calls for which the client paid £1.50 per minute, while the readers themselves were paid £3 an hour. Whether through lack of pecuniary motivation or simple dishonesty, most of these so-called readers did not shuffle the cards or attempt to attune to the client. Many said the same thing to everybody and in all cases their main aim was to keep the caller on the line for as long as possible, for which occasional bonuses were granted. In other words, at least 50 per cent of the people there were fake.

I have also had my cards read professionally, at great expense, and received one particular reading which was as shocking in its omissions as it was in its interpretations. I got the High Priestess as my significator (i.e. representing me in the present) and was told nothing of its profound significance whatever, merely that I was going to move house (which I was not). As a professional Tarot reader myself, I cannot help but be aware that the room for error and misguidance is vast and that sometimes people will receive a reading that puts them off for life.

The million-dollar question is: is one guided from above as to which reader one goes to or which interpretation one gives as the Seer? Perhaps a caller was supposed to be given a bad reading in order to stop them spending £30 a night on their oracle addiction? Perhaps I was subjected to an expensive and unsatisfactory reading in order to be shown how *not* to do it? Certainly this is the most comfortable of conclusions to draw, though it does rather let the charlatans off the hook.

So, bearing in mind that all is not always as it seems – a magickal adage if ever there was one – let us look at some of the genres, titles and techniques of the priestess as Seer. In all cases, it is important to discriminate between imagination and true perception.

THE TECHNIQUES

Psychic Ability

There is nothing 'supernatural' about this quality; rather, it is 'ultra-natural'. So-called 'psychism' refers to perception and we may observe it in enhanced form in some animals (cats and dogs especially), in those who have trained themselves as sensitives and at times of personal crisis or intensity.

A large part of psychism is sympathetic resonance, which might be described as telepathy. Psychic ability is latent in everyone, and involves the accurate reading of situations and people. Sensations and signs are interpreted, often to the 'amazement' of those who are less receptive to the clues available. Psychic ability is a type of 'brain radio'; the adept can tune in to whatever wavelength is suitable at the time. The results may be received clairvoyantly, clairaudiently or simply as a sense of knowing.

Clairvoyance

Clairvoyance is the predominantly visual perception of information. It often involves the ability to physically see spirits, auras, astral entities, God forms and so on. Clairvoyants who work with Magick will 'see' the energies as they interact and cause change to occur. A Tarot reader who is clairvoyant might see the aura of the client and note the way it affects the images on the cards. For example, an animal might suddenly start moving in the image, or the picture of the sea might go from rough to smooth, or one of the characters might shift its position.

The clairvoyant is also likely to receive cinematic views of events past and future, during which the physical surrounds diminish or even disappear and the vision becomes a stronger reality. This is usually active rather than static and may involve symbols rather than mundane scenes, though the latter are also common.

Clairaudience

Clairaudience is the ability to hear via 'brain radio'; that is, to gather information via voices or sounds which are not physically present. This can be one of the most disturbing of psychic phenomena and it has certainly had bad press courtesy of psychopaths who claim to have been told by 'voices' to perform certain acts of terror. Needless to say, there is a world of difference between this and clairaudience. A genuine clairaudient experience will carry with it a spiritual timbre which is impossible to doubt; this really has to be experienced to be understood.

Some psychics receive clairaudient impressions via guides who 'speak' to them or from a source that is consistent but may be unknown. They are also able to hear rather than see when involved in conversations with spirits or God forms.

Music and sound vibrations which are not of the pitch commonly received by the human ear may also be received clairaudiently. This is simply the human equivalent of a dog or a bat picking up on a note of a scale we cannot perceive, or the difference between channels on a radio.

Many musicians do not call themselves clairaudient, yet they pick up tunes and harmonies 'ready-made' from the astral planes. Many composers cannot write as swiftly as they 'hear' the music.

Planets have a particular sound vibration, to which the phrase 'music of the spheres' attests, and each person too has a pitch and note particular to their essence. This was recognized by the Ancient Egyptians, who correlated one's name with one's essence and personal key; thus, knowledge of a name gave complete power over a person.

Mediumship

This term usually refers to the ability to communicate with human spirits after their bodies have died. Mediumship became popular in England and America during the Victorian era and involved such parlour-tricks as table-tipping, knocking (spirit-rapping) and the production of 'ectoplasm' by those claiming to be channelling the dead. While much of this was pure showmanship and manipulation, it is obvious that speaking with the dead is sometimes possible and it certainly forms part of the role of the priestess.

The art commonly known as mediumship often involves giving 'proofs' such as the name of one's grandfather or the colour of one's cat. Of all the 'occult' arts, it is the most prone to abuse, either deliberately or through self-delusion. Some mediums use 'guides' to bring the spirits over, though this is by no means compulsory. I personally find that direct interaction with the spirit is vastly preferable, though certainly more than one entity may turn up at a time and the communication may be far more than two-way.

The most likely scenario for a genuine visitation is when a particular message urgently needs to be given. In my own experience, one such example was a suicide who needed me to write a letter to his wife. Another was an 18-year-old who had been killed in a motorbike accident. He needed to convey a message to his family, who were suffering immensely. In both cases, the communication was spontaneous rather than sought.

It is my personal belief that spirits ought to be either incarnate (physically alive) or on the astral or other planes, unless they are ascended masters or highly spiritual beings delivering messages, and that being tied to or called to the Earth level is not healthy for an ordinary soul. The idea of trying to gain information or guidance through ordinary mediumship strikes me as about as useful as (and far more convoluted than) stopping a random stranger in the street and asking *them* for advice or predictions. These randomly contacted spirits are mostly simply dead humans whose Karma or spiritual and emotional ignorance has left them in limbo. As such, they are to be helped rather than harassed or consulted.

Tools such as Ouija attract the more disturbed of these entities and those who do not believe themselves to be dead. The task of the priestess is to lead these unfortunates to the Light and certainly *not* to earn money or kudos by conversing with them 'in session' or on stage.

There are occasional exceptions to this, which depend on the integrity and talent of the medium. I know one or two people whose classic-style mediumship is certainly to be trusted and seems to be useful both to the 'relative' and the spirit concerned. However, the priestess is advised to work alone or with trusted friends, to employ her common sense and integrity at all times and not to 'call' for a particular spirit. If they want to come, then come they will, when the moment is right.

Witchcraft and Magick

These terms are rather ambivalent, but I use them here to outline oracular and visionary techniques which have developed from schools other than the latter-day manifestations of Victorian Spiritualism (classic mediumship, etc). However, it is to be noted that the Theosophist Helena Blavatsky was well versed in these techniques (some of which she publicly ridiculed) and that her influence has permeated modern Magick and Witchcraft.

As far as oracular and visionary techniques are concerned, I include in the section the invocation of Gods and Goddesses such as Thoth, Mercury, Hermes, Hecate, Isis, Persephone and other visionary energy forms. This is a technique I use personally for my work as a Tarot reader. These divinities increase both one's perception and one's ability to accurately convey the impressions received. As I mentioned earlier, it is essential both to convey empirical information and to flow psychically and intuitively.

Other techniques particular to Witchcraft and Magick as I define them might include the use of certain astral portals (or symbols) as gateways to higher perception and articulation; the association of one's consciousness with various magickal energy patterns (this is a little complex to go into here, but may be facilitated in several ways); the use of familiars to gather information (I know one or two witches who use this rather morally questionable technique); or the acquisition of information via sticks, stones, guts and blood (as in Druidic and

Voodoo divination rites) and other rudimentary tools. Of course, crystals, cards and so on are just more refined versions of the same arts.

Ritual

Very closely associated with the techniques described immediately above, the classic form of oracular prowess is invoked via specific ceremony in accordance with natural rhythms (such as the Full Moon or a holy day), music and drumming, the use of sacred substances, costume and other atmosphere-enhancing techniques. Shamanistic cultures use heavy ritual, as does Voodoo. In modern Magick and Witchcraft too, the priestess is encouraged to become oracular via ritual and atmospherics. The Goddess is drawn into her *(see 'The Charge of the Goddess' in the Glossary)* so that the deity may 'speak'.

Whether a group is present or not, a modicum of ritual is beneficial prior to any sort of divination – at the very least, clearing oneself of extraneous and subjective vibrations and, of course, attuning oneself to the task in hand; that is, invoking focus and clarity.

Bearing in mind these approximate delineations, let us look at the tools which may be employed by the priestess as Seer.

THE TOOLS

Astrology

Astrology is the art of interpreting character and future proclivity through knowledge of celestial statistics at the time of birth. The priestess adept at astrology may well use her intuition (and acquired under-standing) in conjunction with the facts, but astrology is so algebraic in nature that it may be accurately and instantly surmised via any number of websites and other impersonal means.

Personal readings aside, astrology may also be used to determine global and even cosmic events, shifts of energy and so on. A basic knowledge of astrology is highly desirable in any occultist; indeed, some would argue that accuracy is impossible without it. An advanced understanding will allow the practitioner to convey accurate visions and predictions, particularly in conjunction with the intuitive faculties.

Aura Reading

Aura reading is the ability to see and interpret shape, colour, chakric information and so on in the energy body of a person, animal, plant or any magnetized object or being. This is not usually visible to the naked eye (though it is my personal belief that almost anyone can see auras under certain circumstances).

A simple example of aura reading: I went into work once and instantly saw, physically, a black swirling miasma surrounding my boss Charlie. Charlie had no spiritual or psychic involvement whatsoever, yet he was emanating this very tenable aura. I could even see black particles spreading out from him and affecting the room. Somewhat taken aback, I asked him what was wrong. Completely surprised, he admitted that he was in an exceptionally foul mood that day and had just had an argument with his wife over the phone.

Why his aura/my perceptions were so strong that day, I cannot tell, but it was clear that Charlie's emotions were polluting his otherwise lucid or colourful energy body.

Black miasmas are not difficult to interpret; some other colours and formations may be. Some excellent books have been written on the subject *(see Recommended Reading)*, but these should not be seen as definitive guides, as each of us perceives differently, and experience is the true indicator. For example, yellow to some people indicates physical health, while to others it means intellectual ability and/or mystical experience. It is quite possible that one colour may stand out to one psychic and another to a different reader, depending on their attunements. Often an aura contains many colours and shapes. Aura reading is thus best approached first as an overview, then stage by stage up the body, or at least chakra by chakra. Very different results may be received from each. As with many of these divinatory techniques, a trance-like state is helpful to facilitate full perception.

Divination Cards

Cards such as Tarot, Medicine (North American Indian) and Angel cards are the staple tools of many an oracle. Incidentally, there is another set of cards you may find helpful for developing intuition and telepathy: the Zener deck. This contains five sets of five cards, each imprinted with a clear symbol such as a square or a star. The idea is to intuit which symbol you either hold in your hand or your working partner is focusing on.

Getting back to cards used to divine specific situations and the future, there are thousands of excellent Tarot packs available, many of them based on the designs and concepts of the original Rider-Waite pack, which is the one I usually recommend to the novice. Designed by the talented priestess and artist Pamela Coleman-Smith *(see page 29)*, the cards are easy to learn and interpret, and highly susceptible to auric interaction. The pictures often move in accordance with the meaning of the reading (all good packs should do this; of course, it is really 'caused' by the reader and the subject).

The most important thing is to be happy with the imagery of your cards and to find them easy to interpret. Most people begin with a book in one hand and the cards in the other, and there is nothing wrong with this. Although some readers claim to be able to give accurate readings without knowing what the cards actually mean, this seems rather slipshod to me. Intuition is a wonderful thing, but there is a reason for the cards to have specific meanings: they reflect the collective unconscious. A reading should echo the situation of the subject by externalizing the subtleties of their subconscious and Higher Self, bringing light to situations half-perceived and illuminating future possibilities. The role of the reader is to interpret these as accurately as possible, in conjunction with their own intuitive perceptions.

Angel cards have become wildly popular recently. Angels of course do not inspire the same levels of fear which the Tarot can, with its Devil, Death and Tower imagery. Such illustrations can sometimes alarm the subject of the spread. Angel cards also carry the advantage of being more 'acceptable' to the orthodox religions, all of which include Angels in their 'positive' cosmos, whereas the Tarot has been given bad press as 'the Devil's picture book'!

However, the Tarot is far more complex than other divination decks and demonstrates a wealth of wisdom. Of the 78 cards in the deck, 22 depict 'the Fool's journey', an allegory of the spirit's journey through life and its various challenges and initiations. These cards, known as the Major Arcana, have very specific meanings regarding one's spiritual progress, as well as conveying a great many symbols which may be interpreted both empirically and intuitively. The images also act as portals; that is, psychic gateways to specific meditative and magickal wavelengths. They describe an entire incarnation's worth of spiritual development, as well as giving a great deal of psychological and shorter-term information.

Of the 56 remaining Tarot cards, each belongs to one of four suits: Pentacles (Earth/the material), Wands (Fire/the conceptual), Cups (Water/the emotional and spiritual) and Swords (Air/the intellectual and challenging). Each suit has a Page (germinal stage/intermediary), a Knight (concept in progress), a Queen (concept established and developing) and a King (maturity and full establishment). These cards can be used to represent particular people in a spread or can indicate situations.

To each of these suits are attributed 10 Minor Arcana, or stages from I to X. Naturally, each of these has its unique meaning as well as demonstrating a concept or theme in progress. For example, the V Swords not only represents a developmental stage in a psychological issue or intellectual project, but it also denotes rivalry, petty jealousy, and other low-level emotions surrounding the subject. Therefore the card carries a warning against trusting others too easily and against taking pernicious atmospheres to heart.

Obviously the full meanings of the Tarot and other divination cards are too complex and lengthy to go into here, but the reader is directed to the works of Emily Peach and Rachel Pollack *(see Recommended Reading)* for greater elucidation. The potential priestess is encouraged to use the Tarot (particularly) for both meditation and divination, and to explore and develop its fascinating living legacy.

Crystals

The crystal ball is the most popular tool of divination as far as the popular imagination is concerned! In actual fact, it is used far less frequently than cards, rune stones and so on.

The crystal ball, like the magick mirror, tasomancy (tea-leaf reading) and lateral props, is just that: a prop. The medium looks into it with the full power of their intuition and interprets the shapes and symbols they behold. This facilitates a more free-form reading than, say, Tarot, as there are fewer specific meanings to relate. Rather like the surface of the cauldron in *The Wizard of Oz*, prophetic images are sometimes said to play themselves out in the crystal. The same may be said of scrying *(see below)* with magick mirrors.

I-Ching

This ancient form of Chinese divination involves the throwing of yarrow sticks or coins and the interpretation of the Yin/Yang energies indicated by the reading. The answers obtained are usually oblique, symbolic and philosophical in nature.

Numerology

There are many schools of numerology, including a complex branch specific to Qabalah called Gematria. Most basic numerology systems take one's date of birth and name into account and some involve figures as apparently random as one's house number! The results may be used to interpret character and psychological tendencies, and occasionally to predict the future.

Palmistry

Again, there is more than one school of divination calling itself palmistry. One of these involves looking at the most obvious lines in the palm (usually the left) and utilizing the intuitive faculties in order to give a character analysis, short-term prediction or a long-term assessment. (My own experience of this is classic – I visited a fair when I was 14, crossed a gypsy's palm with silver and sat in her caravan with my palm outstretched. I was swiftly told that I would become a doctor and have four sons. None of it came true.)

The other main branch of palmistry is much more scientific and is called Cheirology. This involves the science of the lines in one's palm, including those which are relatively minor. It seems that decent assessments and predictions may be produced via this technique.

Psychometry

This art is definitely psychic rather than scientific! It involves holding an object and receiving auric and vibrational information from it. This is used to access particular entities (such as the previous owner) and to receive impressions from the past and perhaps future, which are then relayed in a form that is hopefully helpful to the subject of the reading.

Psychometry is sometimes used to help find missing persons or even objects. Often 'messages' from beyond the grave are given by the psychometrist through interaction with a particular object. Psychometry may also act as a simple prop for the intuitive and imaginative faculties.

Rune Stones

Runes are an ancient Nordic divination tool (and alphabet), purported to have been obtained by the God Odin after he had hung from the sacrificial tree for nine days and nights. Mythologically, they represent a similar gift to that which Prometheus brought to mankind in Greek myth: fire, or consciousness. They are tools of illumination and prediction, enabling foresight.

As with any tool of divination, the runes carry a particular vibration and mythos which will appeal to some and not to others. They can be as blunt as one might imagine a Norse tribe member to be, yet they can be oblique and require intuition to help with deciphering. The interested reader is referred to the Recommended Reading for further information.

Scrying/Skrying

The word 'skrying' comes from 'to descry', or to tell aloud in divination. The famous Elizabethan astrologer Dr John Dee and his assistant Edward Kelley skryed using a crystal. Kelley would tell what he saw and Dee would act as scribe and interpreter. They also employed necromancy to the same ends – a spirit, sometimes returned to its old body, would be interrogated by the pair on future events and so on.

The magician Abra-Melin the Mage used a seven-year-old boy to the same ends: the child would look into water, under ritual circumstances of course, and announce what he saw.

Other forms of skrying use dark mirrors, animal entrails (the Druids were big on that one) and all of the techniques described above.

Whatever your chosen techniques and tools, it is certain that practice breeds both confidence and competence. Of course, the reading does not have to be for others – it is probably best at first if it is not. Contrary to popular myth, it is fine to buy your own Tarot cards (I did, and believe me, they work!) and also to divine your own future. The only snag is the temptation to veer the interpretation in favour of what is desired (or conversely to see only doom and gloom in the spread).

The best way to avoid subjectivity, at least when learning, is to make a list of meanings and interpretations at the outset and to stick to these when reading for oneself. Intuition may of course be employed too, but with discrimination. Indeed, of all of the tools of the priestess as oracle, discrimination is surely one of the most important. When reading for others, tact and good articulation are also essential. It goes without saying that one should understand one's tools before inflicting them on others (especially professionally!), so *learn*!

Spellcraft

Spellcraft is an act of focused Will. Although this may sound dubious, with its Witchcraft and Voodoo connotations, it is my opinion that all of life is a type of spell-casting. If we fail to focus and our aims and ambitions become blurry and ill-defined, our Spirit has cast a very shoddy spell on our circumstances (i.e. it has failed to aim and fire). If our lives are exciting, progressive and full of love and laughter, the Spirit has cast an adept spell on our lives.

Of course, it is not always as simple as this, as most of us are compromised by material circumstances such as financial concerns, health issues, employment and the situations of others. However, it is certainly possible to optimize one's potential in almost any situation, and this is certainly what the priestess does.

The only real difference between spellcraft and regular willpower is the props that are involved in the process. These are built up in sympathy with the priestess's intent and follow classic correspondences that are well known to the practitioner of Magick.

The most obvious examples of such correspondences are the seasons and the Sun and the Moon. The technique is simple and involves an aspect of what is called 'sympathetic magic'. This means selecting times, events and objects that create a resonance with one's Will – a 'sympathy'. For example, if the aim is the growth and nurturing of a relationship, it would be best to work when the year is waxing (that is, between winter and summer), so that the intent follows the trend of natural growth. The seasons can thus be used as a 'prop' for one's aim. Likewise, one could symbolize such an intent by planting a flower or some such, and watching it grow as the spell comes to fruition (and accepting the symbolism if it either flourishes or dies!).

Lunar currents are perhaps the most important to spellcraft, as the Moon represents the intuitive aspect of life and its tides affect us on both physical (hormonal) and spiritual levels. So, when the Moon is waxing, it is the time to cast constructive, augmentative spells. The Full Moon is the perfect time for insight, clarity and non-subjective workings (for example, divination). The Waning Moon sends the obsolete away on its tides and as such is the ideal time for the shedding of unwanted influences, for whittling away at obstacles, and for any other issues that require diminishments – the antipathy of another towards us, for example. The Dark Moon (when the Moon is not visible) facilitates the breaking of habits and the termination of unwanted influences. It is the dark night symbolic of death, prior to resurrection, and represents psychological and spiritual cleansing.

Solar currents are relevant more to the hour of focusing. Each hour of the day is ascribed to a certain Angel and thus has particular properties (traditionally speaking, at least. It is my personal belief that one's intent can override the bulk of the esoteric statistics).

It makes a big difference psychologically what kind of light a spell is cast in. If cast at midnight by candlelight, it will have a whole different psychological impact than if cast in the fresh light of morning, or at sunset. The twilight hours are infused with magic and allow a liminal atmosphere to be enjoyed by the priestess. This is a time at which realities seem to cross over and anything seems possible. The French call it *entre chien et loup*, as it is impossible to tell in the demi-light what things are, for example whether a quadruped is a dog or a wolf, i.e. a friend or a foe. This imagery is used in many Tarot decks to depict the Moon, a card representing hidden influences, emotional confusion, psychism and convergent realities.

Days of the week are also important to take into account, as each traditionally possesses its own planetary correspondences. For example, a love spell is traditionally cast on Venus' day, this being Friday. A spell or meditation to improve one's powers of communication (or to help with, say, the writing of a thesis) is best performed on a Wednesday, the day of Mercury. A list of basic correspondences is given on page 90.

So much for the timing. Paraphernalia also plays a role in some aspects of spellcraft. Of course, the adept can cast any spell at any time completely prop-free, but the rest of us will probably need all the help we can get. Consequently, we use candles whose colour appertains to our intent. This is not essential, but it can be helpful. For example, yellow is a far better colour to use for healing than black. However, green for healing can represent replenishment and refreshment, for obvious reasons, and as such, some people say it should not be used in cancer treatments, for example, as it encourages replication. The traditional colour correspondences are listed in the table on page 90.

Oils and incense play a huge role in successful spellcraft, which might be compared to a type of self-hypnosis, but with the additional effect of 'hypnotizing' the atmosphere around one. It is well known that certain scents and substances have particular correspondences and effects; for example, frankincense has regal connotations and solar attributes and invests the atmosphere with solemnity and affluence.

Jasmine is associated with pure love, beauty and spiritual bliss, and as such may be used to 'sweeten' any situation. Please see the table on page 90 for some of these correspondences.

So much for the props. But what of the actual act of casting a spell, of causing one's Will to come in effect? How is it done?

We often wish for certain things and sometimes feel determined to bring them to pass. However, these emotions are all too often a flash in the pan and are forgotten a week later. How many people do you know who talk of big plans in business, or of writing a book or play, or some other aspiration, often inspired by a specific mood, or a pint of beer, who never actually *do* anything about it, or if they do, whose attempts are so slipshod that they get precisely nowhere? Spellcraft helps prevent this by focusing personal will (rather than dissipating it with big talk) and by adjusting the surrounding atmosphere to be as conducive as possible to the task in hand.

The techniques are so various that they cannot be fully covered here, but a few of the basics may be discussed.

Candle Magick

Candle Magick is one of the simplest and most effective forms of spell-casting. A candle is made or bought that represents the practitioner's intent – a white one for purification, for example *(please see correspondence chart on page 90)*, a tea light for a brief or devotional spell, a sturdy candle of orange to promote health and wealth in the home.

It is conducive, although not essential, to dress the candle with a suitable oil, or even simply with olive oil. The point is that the candle is imbued with one's intent as one dresses it. This usually involves dipping the fingertips in the oil, then starting at the middle and moving to the ends of the candle whilst concentrating on the aim of the spell.

In a similar vein, a symbol or sigil of one's intent may be carved into the candle with a pin or the tip of a knife or athame (a ritual knife). All of these things help to associate the object with the subject of the spell. When the flame is lit and the Magick starts to unfurl, the candle represents the point of focus between different levels of reality, the point at which the physical level meets the astral (the world of energies behind form).

As the flame begins to wear down the wax, the practitioner envisages their intent in full dynamic visualization. The capacity for imagination is thus employed as an extremely helpful tool. It is well known that 'we are what we think' and we can certainly *become* what we think too. The trick is to imagine (and will) the desired scenario in full detail, navigating one's way through the scenarios in a manner that produces a good end result. Many famous and successful people have used the same technique, though most of them would not call it spellcraft.

This focus obviously takes up a lot of energy and in most cases is not sustainable for the entire time it takes for the candle to fully burn down. Ways around this include working on consecutive days (at the same time each day is good, but not essential), or wrapping the remains of the candle when finished and either burying it or putting it in a box as appropriate (in which case it can be used again to strengthen the spell).

Elemental Spells: Fire and Water, Earth and Air

This type of spell employs the natural elements in conjunction with Spirit in order to affect change. Its modes of operation are various, but follow the 'sympathetic' role model. For example, a habit one wishes to be rid of could be written on a piece of paper and burned, or symbolized by a dead leaf and sent off on a current of water. Some protection spells are buried in the earth for safekeeping and others are written on stone or carved into wood.

It is usual to 'Invoke the Quarters' before a spell or ritual, so that all four elements are present in the ritual. This basically involves asking the spirits of Air (East), Fire (South), Water (West) and Earth (North) to be present and to protect the working. In conjunction with the fifth element of Spirit, this creates a sacred and protected sphere in which to work.

The permutations of elemental Magick are numerous, but it is likely that by using your intuition and imagination, you will deduce how best to symbolize and harness your intent.

Vocal Spells

These involve the use of mantras *(see page 58)* and chants which have a compelling effect both psychologically and on the subtler levels. These can be used alone or in conjunction with any of the other techniques described.

Visualization

This is the most essential ingredient of any spell, which can also be used on its own, even over the washing-up or in the bath! Many people do it unconsciously and it's like a vitamin pill to the Will. Essentially, one 'zones off' into an imaginative wavelength in which 'fantasies' are enacted. The more frequently a particular scenario is envisaged, the nearer and more real it becomes, and the smaller the step into making it a reality. Of course, this works equally with negative thoughts, hence the importance of 'thinking positive'. (Often difficult, I know. Please see 'Facing the Dark Side of the Moon', *page 113*.)

Although such symbolic acts are at worst innocuous and at best successful, I am not suggesting for one moment that all of life's ills can be cured by the simple casting of a spell. For a start, there are thousands of other factors to be taken into account, not least the Will of others. Opposition is rarely insurmountable, but it can at times take a while to whittle it down. Then there is the issue of personal Karma; it may be that we are stuck in a particular position for reasons of spiritual or psychological growth. Perhaps it would be a disaster for us in some way we are unable to see just yet if, say, our novel was published now or we switched jobs.

My personal belief is that we can do as much as possible for ourselves, but that higher forces are in operation and these have a great deal more control than we do. So you could call a spell a kind of focused petition. Even if it's not instantly granted, it at least acts as a target at which we might aim on a long-term basis.

THE SOLAR SEASONS

The priestess does not simply follow the lunar calendar; she is also acutely aware of the cycles of the seasons. The solar year affects magickal and practical issues at too deep a level to be ignored.

In the Western Hemisphere, the year is divided into eight main sections and each holds a particular energy of birth, growth and decline. The obvious analogy is that of nature, but since we are a part of nature,

BASIC MAGICKAL CORRESPONDENCES

Planet	Influences	Perfume	Colour	Day of the Week
Sun	Good health, expansion, wealth	Frankincense, juniper, orange, laurel	Gold, yellow, orange	Sunday
Moon	Magick, intuition, divination, spirituality	Rosemary, sandalwood, myrrh, lotus, jasmine	White, silver, violet	Monday
Mars	Power, dominion, vigour	Tobacco, cumin, High John the Conqueror, allspice	Red	Tuesday
Mercury	Communication, swiftness	Clove, peppermint, lavender	Yellow	Wednesday
Jupiter	Popularity, conviviality	Hyssop, anise, sage	Purple	Thursday
Venus	Love, nurturing	Rose, jasmine, hyacinth	Green, rose	Friday
Saturn	Confinement, discipline	Cypress, patchouli	Indigo, black	Saturday
Uranus	Speech, spiritual guidance	–	–	–
Neptune	Mysticism, spiritual objectivity	Narcissus, seaweed	Turquoise	–
Pluto	Depths of the unconscious, negative karmic issues	Ambergris	Black	–

however sophisticated and divorced from the original state we may consider ourselves to be, it is to be expected that our own energy flows will reflect the seasons and that the manner in which they are operating will affect us on a fundamental level.

The Wheel of the Year operates in a totally logical manner: the period between Winter and Spring is one of germination; Spring brings a powerful uprush of growth and energy; at Summer this energy peaks and begins its decline; Autumn is the time for harvest, reflection and steeling oneself for the hardship to come, represented by Winter. However, the priestess is aware of much more subtle aspects to the Wheel of the Year, as outlined below.

Please note that the dates mentioned refer to the festivals, or Sabbats, in countries in the Northern Hemisphere, which have Summer in July and Winter in December. For New Zealand, for example, the dates will be reversed, so that Samhain will take place around 1 May, Beltane around 31 October, and so on.

The Wheel of Life

Samhain (31 October)

Samhain (pronounced *So-veen*, *Sow-ain* or *Sew-en*) takes place on 31 October or on the nearest Full Moon to it. Also known as Halloween, this is the Western Day of the Dead, its themes being those of interaction across the veil, divination, death and rebirth. Re-incarnational issues take on particular impetus at this time of year. Samhain epitomizes the spirit of autumnal death and potential rebirth. It is the Celtic New Year.

For the priestess, the energies of this time of year may be used extremely constructively. The shedding of unwanted influences, old habits and deep-seated issues is one possible use; a sense of the continuity of past-present-future is also easily accessed at this time of year, giving courage and insight to the priestess as she traverses the 'desert' of the material world. This is certainly one of the most lucid and inspiring times of year for the priestess.

The Goddesses of this most potent of times are those of Magick and divination. Cerridwen the sorceress is one example, Hecate as elderly lady another.

Winter Solstice/Yule (21 December)

The shortest day of the year occurs on the Winter Solstice and yet it is a fire-festival in the midst of the season of ice.

The priestess, following local as well as cosmic energy shifts and peaks, is aware of the need for a sense of hope at this dark time. Nowadays we are still affected by weather and levels of light – indeed, it has been clinically proven that lack of light causes depression as well as illnesses such as rickets (from which thousands of city-dwelling children died in the era of industrialization, owing to smog obscuring the sunlight). So, the idea is to be the vessel of hope, a symbolic soul-torch.

Of course, most of us are now pretty assured on a logical level that the Sun will rise again – a fact not known to our ancestors! That's partly why places like Stonehenge became the centre of innumerable sacrifices to the Gods. We need not go quite that far, but lighting a fire of thanks and faith might be a good equivalent.

The Goddess at this time symbolizes darkness and the passage of time, so Kali is one equivalent. Slightly more local deities include Hecate and the Egyptian Nephthys.

Imbolc (2 February)

Imbolc celebrates the beginning of Spring. It is also known as the 'feast of lights' and celebrates the germination of potential life.

For the priestess, Imbolc is the start of an exciting ascent into the strongest magickal energies of the year – those of new life and growth. Obviously it is an ideal time of year to initiate new projects. Goddesses of this time include Selene, Artemis and Bride.

Spring Equinox (21 March), also known as Oestara

At the Vernal Equinox night and day are perfectly balanced, with the powers of light on the ascendant. This time of year is ideal for turning over a new leaf and taking an enthusiastic leap into the future. After the long dark night of Winter, we know that things can only get better, in the short term at least!

The Goddesses mentioned for Imbolc are also pertinent to the Spring Equinox.

Beltane (1 May)

Beltane epitomizes growth and flourishing. The energies of this time of year are joyful. We 'gather roses while we may'. It is a fertility festival, as is reflected by the phallic symbol of the traditional Maypole.

Along with Samhain, Beltane is one of the most powerful times of year for the priestess.

Goddesses of this time of year are the voluptuous, hedonistic ones and the Goddesses of natural art, such as Venus/Aphrodite, Demeter as nurturer of growth, the Graces and Muses, and elemental deities such as the Nyads and Nymphs.

Summer Solstice (21 June), also known as Litha

This is the peak of the season of waxing and a time to give thanks and have fun. The Goddess Demeter is one of the deities relevant to this festival; she is still pregnant, but clearly about to give birth, i.e. the bounty of the Earth will soon be harvested.

Lammas/Lughnasadh (1 August)

This is a minor point of the calendar of the Wheel of Life, the significance of which should be obvious. Lammas is simply an ongoing celebration of the goods about to be gathered.

Autumn Equinox (21 September), also known as Mabon or Madron

Essentially this is the Harvest Festival. There is a peculiar Magick about this time of year – the light becomes longer, the shadows deepen and the harvest Moon often appears large and low and enchanting over the land.

The priestess will probably find her thoughts and attentions becoming more universal rather than localized. She may feel a sense of higher intelligences drawing near. This of course will lead her up to Samhain, when her role as oracle and diviner is particularly emphasized.

Goddesses relevant to this time of year are those of waning and twilight, including Nephthys and Isis.

THE INVOCATION AND ASSUMPTION OF THE GODDESS

We commonly use the phrase 'stepping into somebody's shoes'. This means assuming their role. Of course, shoes are such personal items, being both sculpted over time by the shape of our feet and attached to our bodies almost wherever we go, that the phrase is an allusion to stepping into the space that contains a person – that is, their aura or energy body. It represents taking on a new set of experiences and perceptions. Look at Dorothy in *The Wizard of Oz*, who has amazing Technicolor adventures when she steps into the red glittery shoes.

When a policeman or a soldier puts on their uniform, they are stepping into a group mind which will enhance both their aura of authority and their access to the collective strength of that body. When a nun steps into her aptly named *habit*, she becomes married to the Church as a Bride of Christ. Partly through this intense interaction and empathy, psycho-spiritual manifestations such as stigmata become possible. Putting on the uniform affirms the collective mind and re-inforces the intent. The person in uniform is not merely wearing the clothes, they are giving up their individuality in favour of a greater force.

The same might be said on a milder scale for those who follow particular fashions – goth, hippy, urban streetwear. The clothes and style promote a certain mental wavelength. Likewise, when a High Priestess draws down the Moon or when a High Priest dons the antlers of Kernunnos, they are stepping into the shoes or the hooves of something much greater – in this case the greatest that is possible, the spiritual space of the Gods.

Invocation is different from assumption, being milder and more objective. It may take place either externally – in the magickal space but outside the practitioner's body itself – or it may manifest inwardly. It is a process of petition, thus of praise and prayer, of appeal for psychological and spiritual inspiration, and of course of religious sublimation and transformation.

Assumption shares many of these traits, but rather than being a process of appeal alone, it elicits a direct experience of the deity and of the state of Being the deity.

So, on the one hand, with invocation we may perceive the deity, we may gain boons, we may interact to an extent. With assumption of God or Goddess forms, as the word implies, we assume the role of the God or Goddess, and thus obtain a more direct experience of the divine vibrations of that God form. Thus, for atmosphere and safe interaction, we may choose invocation. For intense clarity of perception, for insight that would otherwise not be possible and for an atavistic experience of the deity, we may select assumption.

The sceptic of course will scoff at the idea of employing ancient verse and prayers from civilizations long-dead in an attempt to link with a force they would consider, at best, to be the product of superstition. I respond that it does not matter whether the entity is 'real', an independent being or part of the subconscious, collective or individual, an archetype or even an illusion. The point is, Magick works, and invocation and assumption also work. They are effective as psychodrama and are like spiritual growth hormones to the receptive witch and occultist. They help us to touch the realms of the Divine.

Most religions rely on intercession, perhaps with a bit of evocation – bells and smells – to aid the process. But the magickally-minded are not content to be merely the subjects of the Gods. It is in our nature to seek a closer knowledge of the Powers That Be, a personal interaction with them. As we attest via the Witch's Pyramid* or the third Power of the Sphinx,* we Dare. We dare to be different. Hopefully without being like Icarus and soaring too close to the Sun, we seek to bask in the warmth and vibration that is the Goddess. It is the entire point of the occult, as I see it at least, to be an epiphany-seeking missile. The invocation and assumption of various deities are not essential to this task, but it may well help elevate us fast. And that is something that any seeker after divinity will appreciate.

As the modern priestess is well aware, there are countless mythologies and deities known to the practitioner today. The most popular seem to be Celtic and other Northern pantheons, plus the esoterically ubiquitous Greek and Egyptian, but the Gods worked with magickally are also Tibetan, Japanese, Chinese, Hindu, Slavic Oceanic ... They may still be actively worshipped in temples across Asia or their physical representatives – the statues and altars which we use to approach the energy – may have been reduced to relics in the British Museum. It doesn't matter which. The point is that the Spirit, and thus the channel, remain.

Each deity carries its own group vibration – the deities of Ancient Egypt, for example, are considerably more magickally adept and Death-and-Eternity related than those of some of the more primitive civilizations. Within that group vibration, each deity carries its own implications, its own specific inroads to the Divine. We are lucky enough to be able to select, by intuition and via education, the channel by which we are most likely to attain our ends.

Personally, I most like to work with the Gods and Goddesses of Magick, Sex, Death and the Underworld – in Greek terms, Hecate, Eros and Thanatos; in Hindu, Kali and Shiva – because these elicit the most effective response in me. Other practitioners, however, are drawn to the vigorous Gods of Norse mythology or work effectively with the more refined deities such as the nine Muses – Dame Olivia Robertson of the Fellowship of Isis being an example of one who works effectively with these.

With so many deities to choose from, as it were, we may surmise that their applications are numerous. We may roughly group the Gods by purpose into those of: agriculture and procreation (the nature deities), hearth and home, material enhancement, healers, war deities, love deities, Gods and Goddesses of death and the underworld and those of scholarship, Magick and inspiration.

We not only gain boons and insights from the Gods – we may use them to heal archetypal wounds, a theory put forward and developed in Peter Lemesurier's book *The Healing of the Gods (see*

Recommended Reading). Lemesurier presents the positive traits of a selection of deities, then their flip-side, and suggests 'naming and welcoming' the deity through visualization and use of symbol and then absorbing the positive.

For example, Persephone as a negative displays gullibility, proneness to abduction and rape, possible frigidity, possessiveness, strong subconscious urges, winter depression, manic depression, periodic insanity and obsession with death. The positive qualities of the Persephone archetype include, according to Lemesurier, feminism, graciousness, faithfulness, regenerative and restorative powers, mercy, the ability to learn to love what she originally hated, vulnerability to the spiritual or divine (perhaps the words 'perception of' would have been more precise), and eventual acceptance of death as a part of life. The theotherapy suggested for this Goddess, with her symbols of black poplar, willow, aspen, pomegranate seed, the Moon and the flaming torch amongst others, is to: 'Name, imagine and welcome the lost daughter of Demeter and unwilling Queen of the Underworld; cosmology; self-transformative initiatives; self-development courses; springtime; light; adoption; the Moon; sacrifices of black rams and ewes [OK, we may have to waive that one!] and mint (consult a reputable herbalist).'

We can see from these instructions that the author is suggesting channels through which the besieged innocence and freedom of Persephone in her many manifestations might find constructive expression. This is a psychotherapeutic rendering of what the occultist undergoes via the assumption and invocation of the Gods.

It is important to remember that the assumption of the Goddess should not be undertaken lightly. If so, it will either simply not work, and you will be worshipping an idol, or you will be guilty of *hubris*, which never goes down well with the Great Ones (particularly the

Greeks). Also, Goddesses such as Kali are so mind-blowingly powerful and often challenging (it being her nature) that complacency is bound to be shattered by her presence, particularly with assumption, which is a form of possession, though if done correctly it does not so much override as enhance personal consciousness.

Nor should an assumption – in particular – be approached without prior preparation. It takes a strong psychic constitution to hold the essence of a deity. Esotericists such as Alice Bailey and Dolores Ashcroft-Nowiki have warned of the effects on the endocrine system and the potential imbalances caused by overcharging the psycho-physical circuitry. The same might be said of many forms of Magick, of course, notably chakra and kundalini work.

I do not believe the vessel of the advanced priestess to be in any danger – and by 'advanced', I mean those who have received magick-al training in other lives as much as in this – but assumption it is not neophyte stuff. Apart from anything else, the physical symptoms of a successful assumption can be alarming – hot flushes and spontaneous up-rushes of energy, faintness, disorientation and sometimes loss of consciousness. For this reason it is preferable to have at least one other person to hand when assuming a God or Goddess form. However, invocation maybe safely performed by anyone at any level. Using this technique, we perceive only as much as we are able to perceive and thus our psychic constitutions are safe from harm.

How to Assume Goddess Form

We begin by studying the deity and by finding out as much as we can about her. The intellectual link is not to be underestimated – it creates a platform from which to operate, and by saturating ourselves in knowledge of the one to be approached, we prepare the way for an actual presence. We also ensure that our timing and paraphernalia are accurate in import.

As with all Magick, mood and timing are key factors. We may refer to our table of correspondences *(see page 56)* in order to deduce which season, which day of the week and time of day or night is appropriate to aid the manifestation of our allotted deity. For example, prior to approaching a death-related deity such as Persephone or Kali, we might take a walk in a cemetery (somewhere gothic such as Highgate in north London being ideal), or in order to contact a solar deity, we might arise before dawn and greet the Sun as it rises with incense and a ritual. For Aphrodite, a luxurious bath with candles and music always works wonders. It's a classic trick played out on a minor scale by every woman preparing for a hot date.

We cannot always pick our season, but it is obvious that barren deities such as Hecate are best approached in Autumn/Winter, while Aphrodite for example is a Spring/Summer Goddess. The best results are obtained by picking a Sabbat *(see page 90)* to which the deity is pertinent – thus, the most energetic invocations of the Nymphs or Muses take place at Beltane. It's logical.

Lunar cycles are also of relevance to assumption and invocation, as to every aspect of the priestess's craft. For Isis in her positive aspect, for example, we would aim at a Waxing or Full Moon. For Hecate, the Dark of the Moon is more apt. Even if we are working during the day, the stage of the Moon is affecting our Magick.

There are sometimes specific days which are best for each Goddess form, because of course, each day has its planetary correspondences, as do most Goddesses. Thus, for example, Goddess of love such as Aphrodite is best accessed on a Friday. However, the most important factor is one's mental state. The magickal sphere, after all, is timeless, and within it, the priestess creates her own Universe.

Props and enhancements can be helpful. As previously mentioned, there is costume, for example. Though not essential, this is a helpful tool for the priestess, as it enhances the sense of ritual and purpose. It is worth bearing in mind that many of the world's most effective priestesses have been trained or are naturally proficient in the performing arts. Look at the early Golden Dawn – most of its members were actors, artists and writers. Look at Moina and Samuel Mathers giving live performances of Isian rites on stage in Paris, at Aleister Crowley with his penchant for high drama, sonorous vocalizations and dressing like the Mage that he was. Even Dion Fortune used to sweep around London in a Morgan Le Fay cloak towards the end of her incarnation. These occultists were already powerful, but expressing their power sartorially increased it. It caused others to perceive it, and thus had the knock-on effect of increasing the confidence and defiance of the practitioners themselves.

Worn in the privacy of the Circle, magickal garments serve to focus the mind, to attune the practitioner to a specific purpose – perhaps symbolized by a headdress, or a sigil at the centre of the forehead – and to create a new reality, a reality in which the practitioner operates as fully-functional priest or priestess of the Gods.

Then there is lighting – always important in ritual. Nocturnal workings of course provide the best backdrop for these – candles and even coloured bulbs can create a pregnant atmosphere before the Magick has even started.

Music and sound also prepare and enhance an atmosphere – everything from thrash metal for a hex-breaking ritual to AUM, which may be employed in any working.

Incense completes the preparations. Obviously this should be selected in accordance with the correspondences of the deity.

The following techniques do not apply exclusively to the assumption of God or Goddess forms. Other states of consciousness may also be assumed, in shamanic style, from those of the elements – Earth, Air, Fire, Water and even Spirit – with which the Wiccan priestess will be familiar, to those of various animals, minerals and metals, to heroes and even other living personalities. The latter may be used to great effect, though it is an area which ought to be approached with caution. (Do you really wish to mix karmic currents with an unknown quantity? Or with *any* other? Do you wish to raise the possibility of compromising yourself and possibly the other person? If done at all, this exercise should not be performed too often.) It is, however, an effective way to crack any cryptogram of consciousness – by merging with it.

And so to the actual process of approaching of the Goddess.

As at the beginning of any ritual, we start by creating our sacred space. This is facilitated by the Casting of a Circle (if you are a witch) or the Lesser Banishing Ritual of the Pentagram and the Banishing Ritual of the Hexagram (if you are a ritual magickian). If neither, you can create a sacred space as you deem best.

This process is followed by a spoken or thought oration on the specific Goddess. It is the Great Voice* which is required, not the spoken, which is good for those of us who do not wish to be overheard. The Great Voice, however, should be thunderous and vibrant. At this point, the priestess outlines her intent to the Universe and invites the deity to enter the Circle, and her body too in the case of assumption. Indeed, she *tempts* the deity with the scents, sounds and praiseful phrases which are the most piquant to her. These lines may be drawn from ancient paeans or scribed by the priestess. The point is for them to have personal import and emotion, which leads to a specific mental and emotional connection. The rest will follow naturally. The most important thing is to create a geomantric temple, as it were, for the Goddess to enter and inhabit.

The next thing we need to establish is an emotional rapport with our chosen deity. We have already formed a mental one through studying the history and factual background of the Goddess and through the words we use to evoke her. Now we seek the astral connection of Love. This is essential to an effective working. We must stimulate the heart chakra and offer it as a temple to the Goddess.

This may be done in a number of ways. First, we may envisage a sigil or symbol of the Goddess, such as, for Demeter, the symbol of Venus placed in a heart (see the Rider-Waite illustration of the Empress for an excellent example of the imagery of Demeter). We invest this symbol with energy by imagining it placed over or in our hearts. From there, we *grow* it. We increase our energy input, and as we do so, we witness the sigil or actual image increasing in size. It overtakes the bodily peripheries and soon fills the immediate space around us. It then expands, hopefully of its own accord, and in conjunction with our Will, until we can see it encompassing the whole area we are working in, then the whole country, world and eventually Universe.

We may also summon the energy using intonations, mantras, chants and specific key vibrations. AUM is universally effective, especially when resonated in the throat and Great Voice simultaneously.

When the energy peaks, it is best to perform a small ritual act to curtail its expansion and effect on the priestess, such as folding the arms to seal the aura, or making a lateral gesture of closure. This may be spontaneous or determined before you begin.

Finally, what is left is to absorb the energy into the system. The priestess basks in it, perceiving its special qualities and possibly attaining insights and an inner narrative in the process. This could happen in a flash or take an hour or more.

When this process of absorption has been completed, she thanks the deity and closes the Circle or performs another Lesser Banishing Ritual of the Pentagram. Some practitioners banish the deity, which personally I consider rude and unnecessary. A 'thank you' and maybe *bhakti* seem far more apt. After all, one does not invite friends over for a while and then tell them to leave – even more so the case for a deity.

The end of the process and return to normal consciousness are a cue for renewed humility. Not the servile humility of, say, Abra-Melin the Mage,* in the style of Judeo-Christianity, but a healthy awareness of one's unique place in the Universe. While the Gods exist in the Supernal Triangle, we inhabit Malkuth.*

The return to the realm of our ordinary lives may be simply concluded by stamping on the ground.

DRAWING DOWN THE MOON

In most magickal practices, the Moon represents the Goddess *in toto*. This is not to say of course that all Goddesses are lunar, or indeed that all Gods are solar – for example, Chandra of the Hindu mythos is a male lunar God, as is Ganesha. Ameratsu of Japanese myth is a solar Goddess.

However, it is commonly accepted that the Moon is Goddess-related, 'feminine' and intimately connected with intuition, Magick and divination. The Moon creates light which is pliant and liminal; solids lose their definition in moonshine. Without the normal referents to guide us, anything seems and becomes possible.

Drawing Down the Moon is a form of both invocation and assumption. The priestess attunes her thoughts to this symbol of the magickal arts, to its mythos and meaning, and invests her body and spirit with its properties.

This usually takes place during group ritual and once the energy has been absorbed, the priestess becomes the living representative of all lunar Goddesses. Dion Fortune writes much about this in her novels *The Sea Priestess* and *Moon Magic* (both of which I thoroughly recommend), and explains how the wavelengths produced can be used to push open the doors of perception for all involved and reveal the mechanics of the Universe behind the obvious. This, of course, is one of the main roles of the priestess.

Lunar Magick is used primarily to enhance intuition and spirituality. It is the key to discovering the purpose of our incarnations.

Drawing Down the Moon is of course an assumption of the lunar Goddess form. After attuning to whichever of the lunar Goddesses she feels most at one with at that time, or to a more generalized version, the priestess allows the power of the deity to take over.

In Wiccan lore there is a beautiful piece of poetic prose known as 'The Charge of the Goddess'.* No, it's not Kali or Durga going into battle, it's a statement of kindness, love and truth which the priestess normally recites *if nothing else possesses her*. You could call it a safety net in ritual. It may be improvised or even ignored at the point at which the priestess becomes fully invested with the power of the Goddess.

So, how is it done, exactly?

Well, as might be expected from a technique that pertains to the arts intuitive, the ways and means are many and various, and are certainly open to spontaneity and improvisation. Indeed, this is vastly preferable to following a set ritual. However, there are of course certain basic techniques around which one might work.

The Drawing Down of the Moon is best facilitated when the Moon is visible. The most appropriate stage of waxing or waning depends on which aspect of the multi-faceted Goddess one wishes to invoke.

The first quarter relates to the Maiden, who is usually symbolized by youthful Goddesses such as the Greek Selene. Workings involving this aspect of the Goddess would be on fertility, physical or creative themes; the blessing of newly-weds, children and new projects, for example, and anything else pertaining to freshness and youth.

The most common time to draw down the Moon is when it is full – as 'The Charge of the Goddess' states: 'If ever you have need of anything, and better it be when the Moon is full ...' This time of the month is ideal for magickal ritual of almost any sort. These relate to the Goddess as Mother and priestess, imparter of life and knowledge. She is most often represented as Isis.

The Waning and Dark of the Moon belong to Hecate, the crone, and to all Goddesses of dark Magick, the removal of obstacles, sorcery and lateral wavelengths.

However, all of these themes are adaptable and one certainly does not have to stick to the established themes and patterns to attain a powerful result.

Here is one framework around which to improvise:

Select a time of the month that befits your aim. The Full Moon usually works to any ends.

- *If you can work outside, go to a place you know to be safe and from which you can see the Moon.*

- *Cast a Circle.**

- *Stand with your legs comfortably apart and your arms outstretched, straight and high, in the direction of the Moon. Breathe deeply and evenly, drawing in the power of the Moon and the night with every breath.*

106

- Feel the Goddess entering every cell of your body, investing it with ancient power and strength. You might like to vocalize your intent at this point or ask the Goddess to help you in your endeavour.

- Then, simply go with the flow. You really can't go wrong with this one. On one level you are attuning to the most intuitive aspects of yourself. On another, you are allowing yourself to become a conduit for celestial energies.

- When the energy has peaked, you should feel utterly recharged and on a visionary high.

- Take your time, close your Circle and 'do as thou wilt'.

THE FIVE FACES OF THE GODDESS: THE PRIESTESS'S LUNAR CALENDAR

Although the Moon is not exclusively 'feminine' in nature, a great many female deities have been associated with it since ancient times. In the Tarot, similarly, the highest archetype is the High Priestess, whose symbol is the Moon. She represents Magick, esoteric lore, intuition and spirit itself.

The Moon itself divides into four distinct faces, of which contemporary Witchcraft usually recognizes only three. The three popularly recognized and revered faces are those of New Moon (Maiden), Full Moon (Mother) and Waning Moon (Crone). However, this ignores the Dark Moon and so is incomplete. The fourth face, the Dark Moon, is subliminally associated with negative or demonic workings, hence its omission, but the modern priestess is perfectly capable of using these potencies to positive ends. Indeed, the Dark of the Moon represents the time at which the priestess is at her most powerful, and as such, it seems foolish to ignore it.

The Dark of the Moon is a time of huge creative potential, a stage before manifestation, when the star-spangled sky of Nuit represents the limitless possibilities to which the human soul can aspire. It also symbolizes the menses; while the various other stages of lunation symbolize different stages of fertility, the Dark of the Moon (along with the Waning Moon) is the sterile part of the cycle, and as such is sacred to the barren Goddesses and the aspects of the Crone such as Hecate, Lilith and Persephone as Queen of the Dead.

The fifth aspect of the Moon is what one might call 'the mystery behind the Veil' – to put it Qabalistically, the difference between Yesod* in Assiah* and in Briah* or Atziluth.* That is, it represents the mystical essence behind the physical symbol. Of course, it is this 'hidden' quality which we are working with in all of our operations, but it is not symbolized by any particular face or phase of the Moon. It represents the lunar Goddess *in toto.*

So, the priestess has four visible faces with which to work: New Moon, Full Moon, Waning and Dark Moon. Many ancient calendars were based upon lunar reckoning, with the solar calendar taking precedence much later on. The lunar aspect is much closer to our intuitive and primally religious selves, and it represents a conundrum not present in solar calendars (associated with the faculty of rationale): the fifth aspect, which is outside Time altogether.

The first fortnight is sacred to the Virgin; that is, New Moon to Full. This is the most propitious time for workings for growth, inspiration, initiation and blessing. The Goddesses pertinent to this stage include Selene, Artemis, the Muses and the Graces. As such, the first phase of the cycle brings blessings to arts-related projects.

The next phase is the Full Moon, to which is allocated the symbol of Mother. In fact, one ought to say *expectant* Mother, as the whole point of this symbol is of potential on the verge of being made manifest. Obviously this phase represents creativity, and corresponds with long-term projects. All maternal deities such as Demeter and Hathor are relevant to this stage, as is Isis. Divination is particularly blessed at this time.

The third phase of the lunar cycle is represented by the fortnight of waning, with the energies of growth on the decline and indeed reversing during this time. Magickally, this is the phase at which to work with the energy of riddance – the destruction of bad habits, for example, or the shedding of emotional patterns or relationships that have become obsolete or obstructive. The lunar tide carries unwanted influences away with increasing strength over this fortnight. Hecate, Athene and Durga are amongst the Goddesses allocated to this phase.

The final quarter of the lunar wheel is that of the Dark Moon, and this stage is by far the most potent, magickally speaking. It is the stage which represents Death and Rebirth, and the Goddess form relevant to it is that of the Harlot, whose sexuality is for her own empowerment rather than for procreative ends. This is the best time for works of psychic exploration, sex Magick and other more offbeat pursuits of the priestess. This stage can also produce prophecy and oracular prowess.

In workings, these four phases might each be allocated to a Quarter in the temple, while the fifth aspect, the spirit of the Moon if you will, permeates the entire working from above and below, rather as the principle of Akasha (Spirit) does in elemental workings. It may be viewed as the central axis of the Lunar Wheel.

Receiving the Five-Fold Blessing of the Moon Goddess

Working deosil (clockwise) round the temple, form a Circle of purple and silver flame.

- *Perform a general invocation of the lunar Goddess, asking her, with love and yearning, to lay her kisses – or wounds – upon you. All count as blessings. The kisses themselves may be delivered symbolically by representatives of the Goddess at each Quarter or they may simply be received spiritually.*

- *Begin in the East. Trace a Circle of silver flame, representing the Moon, and at either side of it, an outward-pointing crescent Moon. Surround all of these with another circle, representing the full cycle of lunations.*

- *Within this, visualize a symbol of the Maiden Goddess, such as a sickle Moon. Call her forth and envisage her, perfect and beautiful, young and strong, her milky white flesh inviolate. Perform devotion to this aspect of the Goddess in whatever form you deem fit, until she bestows her blessings upon you.*

- *Move to the South, and stand facing this Quarter of your temple. Trace the full circle, sickle Moons and enclosing circle as before, but at the centre, visualize the Full Moon and the fecund Goddess. Again, aspire towards and worship her until she bestows you with an astral kiss of acceptance and grace.*

- *Next, turn to the West and see there the Twilight Goddess, represented by the cowled and bent Crone. Here, trace the round and sickle and enclosing symbols of the Moon. Envisage the Waning Moon at the centre of it. Honour the sterile Mother, the decay that necessarily precedes growth and new life, the positive spirit of putrefaction.*

- In the North, again trace the lunar symbol, and at its centre visualize the Dark Face of the Moon, representing the Harlot Goddess and the menstrual night, and remain steadfast and focused as you honour this much-maligned aspect of the Goddess's nature. Love is the force which transmutes the poison of her nature (when viewed from a one-dimensional angle) into wine.

- Now, having received the four kisses of the lunar quarters, return to the centre of the Circle and call upon the feminine lunar spiritus that is the central axle of the lunar wheel. Focus on this unmanifest aspect, the true Being behind the symbols, and again, give praise to her. This should bring forth the so-called Negative Kiss, which illuminates and unites the other four.

- You are now empowered to work upon any stage of the lunations. Remember that, as with all magickal scenarios, it is only by embracing both the light and the dark aspects that gnosis may be attained and the Will of the priestess effectively worked.

OBTAINING THE BLESSINGS OF THE SUN DEITIES AND THE SEASONS

Although the priestess works primarily with lunar currents, it is also important to be attuned with solar energies. A simple ritual may be performed using the Four Faces of the Sun – Rising, Midday, Setting and Midnight – to obtain blessings of this more classically male aspect of deity.

The basis is the same as that described above, only this time we will be using the symbol of the Sun in all Quarters. This is usually a circle with a dot at its centre.

The attributes of the first three aspects of the Sun are similar to those of the Moon – Rising is germinal, Midday is manifesting, Setting is declining and the Midnight Sun represents the ever-present solar mythos, the God behind the veil of matter and illusion.

- *Cast a Circle in your temple, of radiant fiery light.*

- *To the East, inscribe the solar symbol in the ether and visualize the Sun rising at its centre. Ask for the blessings of the God in his rising and the Goddess Aurora.*

- *In the Southern Quarter, inscribe the solar symbol and visualize a brilliant midday Sun at its centre. Ask that your eyes may always be open to the Truth and that you might always keep your goals in sight and your motives pure. The Gods of this aspect include Ra, Horus and Apollo.*

- *In the West, make the sign of the Sun and envisage the solar orb as it sets. The blessings to be garnered from this aspect include those of faith, completion of incarnational duties, strength and longevity.*

- *To the North, make the sign of the Sun but this time envisage it as a black circle with a fiery aureole. Ask to be guided in times of darkness, to know strength rather than fear, and hope rather than despair, and for Osiris and Thoth to guide and protect you in times of tribulation.*

- *When you feel the effects of each of these blessings – perhaps arriving as a ray of light perceived with the inner eye, or maybe felt as a physical tingle; we all have our own modes of psychic and spiritual perception – thank the solar deities and close the Circle, carrying the Light forth into your daily work.*

FACING THE DARK SIDE OF THE MOON: NEGATIVE THINKING, DEPRESSION AND SELF-CLEANSING

Bleak though this topic may sound, I felt it essential to include a section on depression in a book on the role of the priestess. Just as the Goddess herself has many dark faces, ranging mythologically speaking from the cool cruelty of the White Goddess of Celtic lore through to the red-hot raging Sekhmet of the Egyptians and the dark devourer, the Hindu Kali, I am yet to meet an effective magickal person who has not been through a Dark Night of the Soul, and often they have undergone many.

There are times when it is almost impossible to attune to spiritual or astral wavelengths. The reasons are numerous. They may be chemical (in the case of many forms of depression), or circumstantial. It's hard to dance with the Devil on your back, and this 'Devil' may take the form of financial concerns, trouble at work, lack of employment, emotional upheaval, bereavement, emotional scarring or simply low self-esteem. How on earth can one think spiritually when beset by debt, or having just been betrayed by a lover or friend, or with a screaming child in the house, to cite just a few examples? It can be difficult to create the personal space, both physically and mentally, which is needed in order to elevate one's consciousness.

There is no sweeping statement that will cure the ills that beset us. Obstacles exist in order to act as foils against complacency and to propel us to greater heights. Very few of these are insurmountable and a personal victory over one or other of them is a gargantuan magickal leap. The uses of adversity are innumerable, but it can be very difficult to see this at the time.

In the Qabalah, the path of the priestess, represented by the Hebrew letter Gimel, is the one which crosses the Abyss. Magickally speaking, 'the Crossing of the Abyss' represents the most extreme of initiations. The word 'Gimel' means 'camel' and the analogy is of crossing the desert, the spiritual wasteland, carrying the water of self-sufficient spirituality on one's back.

The history of the Dark Night of the Soul is vast and mystics of every culture are familiar with it. On a macrocosmic scale, we go through versions of it on a frequent basis. Every irksome situation or challenge is a miniature Gimel-experience.

One aspect to which the priestess is particularly prone is the hormonal: the menstrual or menopausal. Most magickal women are very much under the influence of the Moon and menses. Both are intimately linked, of course. These factors create mood swings and are often accompanied by depressions over which we have very little physical control. The same may be said for those suffering from clinical depression.

The worst thing about these situations is that the material world begins to look like a cul-de-sac and the body a sort of prison. It is all but impossible to think clearly or magickally when under such influences.

Obviously everybody's situation and constitution is different, and there is no great cure-all out there. I can, however, offer a few tips.

First, be kind to yourself. The fact that you have survived this long is a testament to your strength. If you have overcome adversity, unfair treatment and/or depression, you are a survivor. Well done.

Secondly, just because you cannot perceive Spirit at these times, it does not mean that Spirit has ceased to exist. The Hindus call this mode of perception *Maya*, when the material reality of the world seems to be all that there is. *Maya* means 'illusion'.

There are a few techniques you can use to help ease yourself and your body into a better mode of perception. I will leave it to the reader to select or adjust as appropriate to personal circumstances. But these are some of the little tricks I have personally used:

1   *Do something creative. Write or paint, make something or go out and take photographs. It doesn't matter if they're not as good as you would like them to be. You are still developing a skill.*

2   *Take a walk or a more vigorous form of exercise. You might be amazed at the transformation you experience. Best of all, if you can manage it, put on some music you love and dance. This sends 'joy' signals to the brain, which will respond chemically.*

3   *Eat chocolate, the darker (higher cocoa content) the better. Again, this affects the brain, acting as a stimulant for the creation of serotonin, the chemical that creates sensations of happiness and well-being. It really works!*

4   *One of the crystals that powerfully counteracts negativity and promotes well-being is rose quartz. You could meditate with some or carry a bit in your pocket or wear it as jewellery. It can also be used to infuse cold water with its vibrations, simply by soaking, and this water can then be added to your bath. The same goes for other stones and crystals; their various uses are explained in depth in books such as* The Crystal Bible *by Judy Hall (see Recommended Reading).*

5   *Aromatherapy has a hugely positive effect. Scents such as lavender, orange and rose are very uplifting. Some essential rose, orange or lavender oil in the bath or on your pillow at night cannot fail to improve your mindset.*

6   *Ritual bathing is an excellent antidote to depression and mood swings. A handful of salt in the bath cleanses the subtle bodies of psychic dross and unwanted influences.*

Take some in the palm of your right hand while the bath is running and hold it to the East, saying, 'Cleanse and balance me, by the power of Air.' Envisage it glowing with vibrant blue light. Now hold it to the South, saying, 'Cleanse and balance me, by the power of Fire.' See the salt blaze with purity as you do so. Now, hold it to the West, saying, 'Cleanse and balance me, power of Water.' Finally, hold the salt to the North, saying, 'Power of Earth, keep my mind, body and spirit in sacred equilibrium.'

Now throw the salt under the cold tap, visualize cleansing light spreading through the water and get in. Try to 'see' the state of your bodies (psycho-physical, auric and spiritual). How do they look? Allow your recent moods and experiences to inform your perceptions. Chances are, they will not be a pretty sight.

The trick now is to employ the power of the salt and water and of your own will to cleanse and repair yourself. Send healing energy to parts of your bodies which appear broken or sullied, and visualize the dirt, in whatever form it may take, dissolving into the water.

When you are clean and repaired, get out. As the water drains down the plug hole, 'see' your troubles being washed away with it.

I do this every night. It helps to rid me of the heavy emotions and psychic pollution I pick up in my work as a Tarot reader and psychic counsellor and on the Tube. I really recommend it!

7   *Incense is often used in Magick to cleanse and purify. Sage is an obvious example, and rosemary is excellent too. Jasmine promotes an atmosphere of love and compassion, and sandalwood* is handy for grounding and promoting a sense of stability. Waving the smoke of a joss-stick around you (especially if you surround yourself with it) is a simple way of getting rid of influences such as the hostility of others. These subtle, often random negativities can be part of what makes us feel down.

8 Most importantly of all, be kind to yourself. Just because you are feeling down does not mean you are a hopeless case spiritually speaking, or that you cannot be a brilliant priestess. In fact, it is usually indicative of a magickally sensitive person. As any of my friends would tell you, I've spent my fair share of time in the doldrums too, often through circumstance, but also through chemical factors. I can only assure you that the epiphany after the Long Night makes it all worthwhile.

FURTHER FUNCTIONS OF THE PRIESTESS

Healing Oneself

As Philip Larkin put it, 'They fuck you up, your mum and dad.' Mother and father represent the perspective from which we approach life and consciousness. They define our attitudes and thought processes. They are our gateway to the world.

Essentially the moment we enter this world, we are vulnerable to abuse, and if it doesn't happen inside the home, it's bound to happen outside. Physical and psychological damage may be inflicted by accident, oversight or, of course, deliberately. We might find ourselves worsening the situation by projecting our own fear, hurt and confusion onto others and perpetuating the negative behaviour. Whatever the cause, every one of us has an issue to contend with, if not several.

When seen through the eyes of magickal reality, these afflictions are our passport to self-exploration, self-development and the acquisition of life skills. They act as a dynamic energy, the energy of conflict and transformation. They can become a gift of the Goddess if properly treated.

The manner in which the individual approaches the process of self-healing differs widely. What is constructive for one person may not work for another. For example therapy can work wonders *if* you happen to find exactly the right therapist proffering exactly the right treatment, but the wrong person or technique may just make matters worse. I once had the personal misfortune to attend some wildly expensive sessions with a counsellor who did nothing but sip herbal tea for an hour and then tell me that my time was up. Having trained in basic counselling myself, and working as a psychic counsellor also, I feel that a more interactive session is usually much more helpful to the client. A friend of mine spent half an (also rather expensive) hour beating up a pillow whilst screaming at her 'dad' – and that seemed to work for her, though clients with a more pressing sense of dignity may well feel otherwise!

In my opinion, friends and family are often more helpful than professional counsellors might be – even if simply because we have to exercise considerable self-restraint when talking to those we know. It isn't always a good thing to dwell on the negatives, and in my opinion it isn't always a good idea to vocalize them either. Once in a while it is positive, but continual reference to our woes can give them a tighter grip on our imagination and enhance our sense of being unlucky or damaged. The key, as with most things, is in balance.

One step that the priestess may take towards self-healing is to try to see the blessings behind the curses. She may also interpret her experience symbolically and turn her affliction into strength, just as Louise Hay did with her cancer. (Louise Hay is the author of many books on self-healing and the founder of the publishing house whose product you have in your hands. *See Recommended Reading.*) The priestess also tries to be kind to herself and not to make matters worse with masochistic behaviour. Helping others is often a path to self-healing also.

Morality plays a big part in self-healing. If one is lied to, stolen from and abused, the answer is *not* to start lying, stealing and abusing others. I mention this because in my extensive work as a counsellor I have witnessed some people becoming very embittered, while others maintain their integrity against the odds. These people are the ones who make life worth living – the ones with *goodness* inside them. To have this taken, in addition to other issues, is the worst-case scenario. Without ethics, we have nothing in the world to cling to, because if we cannot trust ourselves, we will never be able to trust others, and the world will be a dark place indeed. So, in my opinion, a strong ethical code is an important aspect of self-healing, so important that one might see morality and compassion as selfish! Now there's an amusing thought. However, it is well known that philanthropy makes the philanthropist feel good. Everybody benefits.

So, priestess potential or actual, go out and shine the Light of your Soul in the Darkest places it can reach! That includes your own inner landscape. It's a guaranteed way to facilitate self-healing.

Healing Others

What in the world is better than a good friend? I have no answer to that one. The priestess spreads spiritual healing wherever she goes, and charity begins at home. She is a fabulous friend and, where possible, a supportive sibling and loving daughter. Obviously we all mess up from time to time, but we can but strive, and the craft of the priestess begins on a personality level.

As already mentioned, there are 'personalities' befitting many deities, including those of healing, hearth and home, guidance and friendship, and these are expressed on a microcosmic level by the caring mother, the good friend, the person we all love to have in their lives. And before you go thinking that this couldn't *possibly* be you, with your numerous insecurities, failures and short-fallings, please allow me to assure you that it *is* you, and if not now, then it can become so. This reflects the priestess in the everyday world.

The more conscious priestess is obviously concerned with far wider issues than her own family and friends. She is, after all, the Bridge between Worlds. Her roles include giving psychic and auric treatments to those in need (these will not be restricted to humans, as all things are part of Spirit and contain their own personalities), helping others magickally, acting as a sort of valve in the atmosphere that adjusts its tempo to a higher vibration, developing the relationship between this planet and the Higher Intelligences, and giving accurate and helpful divination which aids the development and enhances the future of others.

The Priestess and the Goddesses

The different faces and aspects of the Goddess are macrocosms of the role of the priestess, and the study and exploration of Goddess mythology, or thealogy, is the most basic of groundwork regarding finding your inner deity and expressing her in your life.

There are far too many Goddesses and demi-Goddesses to enumerate and describe here, so we will begin by looking at Auset, or Isis, the ultimate Goddess of all priestesses, and then at a selection of others according to their particular qualities and associations.

AUSET (ISIS)

Why is Auset so important a figure to the priestess?

First, she epitomizes the energy of all feminine divinity from any culture. She is ancient, the prototype of the Virgin Mary, and her energy is another expression of that of the Hindu Goddesses Radha, Laxmi and Durga combined, likewise of Goddesses from other pantheons. This is by no means to diminish the roles of the other deities, but Auset is one of those who can represent the Goddess *in toto.*

As a Goddess of Magick and spellcraft, anything is possible for Auset in the world that she created for us to inhabit. According to Egyptian lore, it was Auset who made a civilization out of the raw humanity created by the male Gods; she is responsible for animal husbandry, agriculture and, along with Maat, law and order. However, this is far more than a simple set of rules and regulations. It is magickal justice and spiritual symmetry. She is 'the Lady of the Words of Power' – having tricked her uncle Ra into revealing his name (i.e. essential vibration), she was able to strip him of his secrets. This may sound rather a strange metaphor, but Ra had become, according to legend, a despotic and temperamental God – he was the Sun God – and Auset, Lady of the Moon, tempered his wrath with her cleverness and magickal powers. Auset's myth translates as knowledge of the power of creation, used to positive ends. So we have a wily female deity who acts as patron of the magickal arts – clearly of direct benefit to the priestess.

The major roles of Auset involve magickal protection, healing and the arts of fruition and growth. She may be approached for healing, particularly of the etheric and spiritual bodies, in which the problems are usually karmic and abstract; that is to say, psychological or spiritual blocks which hinder one's progress. For example, if every time you hit a particular point in meditation you encounter distracting or scary imagery, Auset is an excellent deity to approach for an explanation and the opportunity to karmically re-adjust yourself. Issues which you know or suspect may be from other incarnations can also be addressed with the help of Auset. The processing of these issues at root level often has surprising effects on the physical body too, which responds to the etheric and mental blueprints by which we design it, i.e. our fundamental energy levels.

The most famous of Auset's myths is the seeking and healing of her husband Asar (Osiris)'s scattered body, which had been chopped into

13 pieces by his jealous brother Set. Flying as a kite (some sources say swallow) across Egypt with her sister Nepthys, she discovered all but the phallus of Asar. Through the use of sacred spells and incantation and ritual, she managed to revitalize Asar to the extent that he was able to impregnate her with the seed of his avenger, Heru (Horus). Thus Auset is the Goddess of restorative love, redemption, healing and protection from harm, particularly from harm caused by the occult arts. Once Heru is born she spends her entire time striving to nurture and protect him as his uncle Set attempts to do away with him by hook or by crook.

Auset is also a celestial sky Goddess and one of the animals most sacred to her is the wild goose, her own equivalent of the Moon God Djehuti's ibis (also white). In Egyptian art, Auset is often shown with wings, which frequently fold around others in a gesture of protection. To be in the sphere of Auset or Isis is to be utterly protected and she will never refuse her guardianship and healing to one of her children, particularly one of her priestesses. She is thus the ultimate antidote to the negative energies that any spiritually active person evokes, for every action has its equal and opposite reaction, and we live in a world of duality. To move forward positively, to shine light into this world, to channel the Magick of the Goddess will inevitably attract destructive energies both astral and human – such as jealousy, spite and challenges from the inner planes. However, if we approach Auset and ask for her protection, her cleansing and her help, we are invulnerable to assault on the personal as well as the astral and physical levels. This is perhaps symbolized by Auset's nurturing of the crippled aspect of Heru, known as Harpocrates.

As a Goddess of Magick and the Moon, Auset also controls all waters, particularly the oceans, and the hidden, psychic tides that affect us all on so many levels. In Ancient Egypt she was closely associated with the flooding of the Nile Valley, which was essential to the prosperity and growth of the crops and therefore populace. In connection to this, she is powerfully connected with the star Sirius, also known as Sothis or the Dog Star, which rose prior to and was considered to induce the flooding of the valley. Hence, in part, Auset's connection with the powers of fruition. Her husband Asar was the God of fertility itself and his disappearance and re-appearance in the Underworld follow an obvious seasonal pattern.

Water itself represents emotion, the subconscious, psychism and spirituality, hence in part the power that Auset has over it. In ancient days her devotees would sleep in her temple in the hope of being blessed with prophetic, healing and guiding dreams. This remains a highly appropriate way to approach this Goddess – by actively asking for help via healing dreams. Trance work is also suitable to this Goddess (and indeed, to most deities). Helena Blavatsky, one of the ultimate Isian priestesses, is said to have spent a great deal of time communing with the Goddess via hashish, and indeed, Dion Fortune's character Wilfred Maxwell in *The Sea Priestess* first encounters the healing energies of the Moon while in an altered state caused by asthma and morphine. There are plenty of ways to approach a state of enlivened spiritual consciousness without such drastic measures (dance, purification diets, mantras, herbal smoking mixtures and teas, music and so on), but it should not be ignored that the Gods and Goddesses have traditionally been approached through the intercession of mind-changing substances ever since they were first worshipped. It simply throws the doors of perception open faster.

The word 'Auset' means 'throne' and the symbol of the Goddess is the same. There is much reference to the 'Veil of Isis', and its lifting, in magickal lore. What lies behind the Veil of Isis? Well, that is for the individual initiate to find out! But one obvious analogy is the Veil as dense, physical matter, the equivalent of *Maya*,* and Isis as the energy and spiritual truth behind it. Auset is both Nature and Nurture, both free-flowing and ritualistic. Her roles are so many that it is barely surprising that she has come to represent all Goddesses.

The scents sacred to her are jasmine, rose and cedar, and all lunar herbs, such as rosemary. As well as the aforementioned wings, another symbol of Auset is the Ankh, the symbol of all life.

In her novels *The Sea Priestess* and *Moon Magic (see Recommended Reading)*, Dion Fortune describes the many functions of the modern-day priestess with particular reference to Isis, and I cannot recommend these wonderful novels (and Dion Fortune's other works) highly enough to the aspiring priestess! They describe a prototype and are highly entertaining as well as informative. Perhaps the entire ethos might be summed up by these words from *The Sea Priestess*:

> *O thou that wast before the earth was formed –Ea, Binah, Ge.*
> *O tideless, soundless, bitter sea,*
> *I am thy priestess, answer unto me.*
>
> *O arching sky above and earth beneath,*
> *Giver of life and bringer-in of death,*
> *Persephone, Astarte, Ashtoreth,*
> *I am thy priestess, answer unto me.*
>
> *O golden Aphrodite, come to me!*
> *Flower of foam, rise from the bitter sea.*
> *The hour of the full moon-tide draws near,*
> *Hear the invoking words, hear and appear –*
> *Isis unveiled, and Ea, Binah, Ge!*
> *I am thy priestess, answer unto me.*

Ideas for Approaching Auset, Ultimate Goddess of the Priestess

There are no set rules for approaching any deity and a personal take on it is usually of vast benefit. However, it is obvious that the use of appropriate correspondences will be hugely beneficial. This could take the form of ritual cleansings, clothing, scents, colours, props and waters, such as, for Auset, lunarized sea or sacred well waters (which have been left to charge under moonlight).

One may follow a prescribed ritual, such as Drawing Down the Moon, with special reference to Auset, or one might simply mediate on her symbols and open the mind to receive interaction. The following very simple guidelines may be used as a basic structure:

1 *Spend some time reading up on the myths of Auset/Isis and contemplating her symbols. This helps attune the mental/intellectual faculties, which for many of us are prone to set up a block unless they are utilized in a positive manner. It also helps the subconscious begin the process of accessing the wavelengths of the Goddess through her symbols. The image of an Ankh, for example, has an effect via the collective unconscious and individual long-term memory (many of us will have associations from other incarnations).*

2 *Gather the props that you feel you would like to use. Examples for Auset range from a flowering jasmine plant to rose oil, cedar chips (to use as incense), candles (silver, purple or rose), lumps of red carnelian (sacred to Auset) and all things associated with water and the Moon. Obviously, Ankh and lateral ancient Egyptian imagery will also be of use.*

3   Create an altar to the Goddess. Place on it the items you have selected for your Isian ritual.

4   It is often said that the best time to work with Auset is at the Full Moon, and this is certainly a highly powerful time. However, as with all deities, it is Will and natural magnetism which draw them to you, so this is not essential. Personally I have worked with Auset right through the Dark of the Moon, and although the interaction tends to have an emphasis different from those of the waxing and Full Moons, it still works. It might even be said that the Dark Moon is particularly helpful regarding protection during crisis and guidance when it is most needed. So work when you are comfortable and attuned.

5   Take a ritual purification bath. Salt in the water will benefit you greatly. Focus on cleansing your bodies on every level, so that when you arise from the waters, you radiate to the inner eye. This is something many priests and priestesses do daily.

6   Dress for ritual, or as you feel most comfortable.

7   Light your incense at the altar and ask Auset to accept the gift of the perfumed smoke and to be with you. Light your candles. Carry the incense deosil around your space so that you create a sacred Circle. Visualize this becoming a sphere of protection.

8   Improvise. You might like to invoke Auset with a hymn or paean, or to pray, meditate on or invoke her in some other way. At this point, the Goddess should take over and your true communion will begin.

9   *Go with the flow. You may have a visionary experience or a heal-ing one. Your perceptions may be visual, clairaudient or both. You may be given tasks or asked by the Goddess to do particular things, either in the Circle or later on. It is often a good idea to write down what you perceive. It may not be in your native tongue, or could appear as a glyph or symbol, and may require analysis later.*

10   *Give thanks and enjoy the Magick!*

If you are naturally attracted to Auset, and if she is your primary deity, you are likely to have at least some of the following traits.

The Priestess of Auset: The High Priestess

This character has much in common with the Persephone archetype *(see page 144)*. She is fascinated by nature as an expression of the hidden Divine, and her associations tend to be lunar rather than solar, as she loves the transformative, liminal effect that moonlight has on the world, challenging our preconceptions and subtly changing our perceptions. Her other symbol is the sea, and of course the two are intimately linked.

The High Priestess has a strong sense of reverence both for the natural world and the sacred of any tradition. She tends to be rather solemn, even as a child, and her strong sense of protocol makes her sometimes appear to others as pompous. She is naturally insular in day-to-day life, but she 'emanates' in magickal situations or at times of spiritual significance.

All followers of the Goddess and of enhanced personal spirituality are priestesses, as we have discussed at length in this book. The reason the Isian archetype is a 'High' Priestess is that she is usually consciously dedicated to her craft and it is of the highest importance to her. The rest of life is correctly viewed as ephemeral.

It goes without saying that this character and her many variations have an active interest in myth and Magick and the many permutations thereof. She works as an active channel of the Divine and as such serves as a role-model to us all.

ARTEMIS

All Goddesses are magickal, but the properties they elicit in their priestesses vary considerably.

While Auset facilitates the sacred in a spiritual sense, the lithe and sporty Artemis of Greek myth is more about personal strength, athleticism and being part of nature. She is as tomboyish as her twin brother Apollo is effete and like all Greek deities she sets out to triumph in any situation.

Artemis is the huntress, the Goddess of the wild chase. Like several other female deities she refuses to marry, guarding her independence and chastity at all costs. She already enjoys a state of near-androgyny, at least sociologically speaking, and as a daughter of Zeus she is naturally invested with power. This she transmutes into the ability to pursue her own pleasures – very literally, as she runs through the forest with her bow and arrows to hand, tracking down the animals that it is her favourite sport to slay.

Before the vegetarians amongst us become aggrieved by Artemis' chosen recreation, may I point out that she is performing just this: re-creation. As the maiden and a representative of the primary life-force, she symbolizes the natural force that slays, that allows nothing to over-reach its prime, in order that life may be renewed and reactivated. Bear in mind that the era in which Artemis was actively worshipped was one of natural abundance, as opposed to now, when the environment and even some of its species are terribly depleted, and of course her era was one in which food had to be hunted and gathered personally unless one was particularly wealthy.

So, by chasing the wild animal to its death, Artemis symbolizes the prerogative of Time, and as such may be said in a subtle way to represent this faculty. While she is immortally young (representing the constant rejuvenation of life), the 'lesser' species, which includes humankind, perish temporarily under the 'slings and arrows' of natural decline.

On a more general level, however, Artemis may be worked with to enhance physical prowess, to increase self-protection and, for women particularly, to guard against encroachments on one's chosen path, particularly if conventional marriage is not desired. Artemis is a deity with much appeal to the woman who prefers other women; to the archetypes, indeed, described below.

The Priestess of Artemis: The Iron Maiden

This young woman (young in stance even if she is physically not) is boyish, determined to succeed in her endeavours and usually sporty. She is the modern Greek *kouroi/kore*, androgynous in looks and style, practical, and fiercely proud. Mythologically, she relates to Artemis and Diana and bears their torch in the modern era. She is feminist, constitutionally and usually overtly. She fights for women's independence and is a priestess of personal liberty. Every priestess has an aspect of Artemis about her, simply through being self-defining.

The iron maiden priestess is excellent at mixing physical exercise with a sense of the sacred. To her, the body is a temple, and she gains contact with her higher self and the Creative Intelligence through being part of nature. Thus, running or swimming outside are particularly good for her spiritually. She loves to compete. She makes a wonderful Dianic Wiccan.

DURGA

The Hindu Goddess Durga is a fine example of female deity as warrior and protector against evil.

Durga is an exquisitely beautiful delicate-looking Goddess who rides upon a tiger or occasionally lion. She wields weapons in her four fragile-looking hands and has a sweet smile on her face. However, this guise conceals one of the fiercest and strongest deities. Created by the other Gods to fight the buffalo-demon Mahisha, who was pestering man and God alike, Durga was invested with the power of righteous fury. In her battle aspect, she has a great deal in common with the Hindu Goddess Kali.

Durga has parallels in other cultures, which I would like briefly to explore here, as it is certain that her mythos affected these more Northern manifestations, but most importantly, it demonstrates that the fighter priestess has long been a part of popular worship. Bearing in mind the history of the priestess, and the fact that these virile female archetypes vanished from Western lore between Joan of Arc (herself a rare example) and the suffragettes, one might well wonder to which sociological prison these and other strong feminine role-models were consigned.

Most pantheons contain at least one Goddess whose role would classically be interpreted as masculine. In Western mythology we have the warrior Goddess Anraste, also known as Andrasta or Andred (whose various forms and nomenclatures are Anglo-Celtic, Romano-Celtic and continental European). Her presence was invoked prior to battle. The army of Queen Boudicca worshipped Andraste and made much blood-sacrifice to her, including the lives of the Roman women of Londinium after the city was sacked by their army. The name 'Boudicca' means, simply, 'Victory'; quite possibly she epitomized a form of the Goddess to her people, making her the equivalent of the Greek Goddess Nike. Both Andraste and Boudicca represent the mythos of the warrior Goddess.

The Irish equivalent is the Morrigan, whose name means 'Great Queen' or 'Phantom Queen', and who manifests both as a single and a triple Goddess. In the multiple she is Badb/Macha ('the Crow'), and Nemian ('Frenzy'). The crow is equivalent to the raven that symbolizes Andraste. The Norse version of the warrior Goddess is the Valkyries, who are also airborne scavengers who preside over battle and death through conflict.

In India, as already mentioned, we have Kali and Durga. There are others of this ilk, many of them far more terrifying and skilled in action than their male equivalents.

Let us focus on Durga. How could such a soft-skinned, smiling, delicate Goddess possibly be attributed with such an incredible ability to slay that she is rumoured to have been created primarily for this purpose? So, I imagine, her legendary suitors may have asked as they met a sticky end on the blades and hooks of her various weapons. This is certainly the last thing the average male would expect at the hands of the divine feminine – after all, aren't women and Goddesses supposed to nurture and protect, to bless and grace, rather than to maim and slay?

I think it may be safely conjectured that part of Durga's legend springs from men's innate terror of the power of beauty. Beauty leads men into sticky scenarios in every epoch. Of course, one may say the same about women being lured by men (though often their beauty is not comparable; the glamour originates rather more from promises of futurity than temporary gratification). Durga, like the Naiads and Sirens of Greek myth, lures men to an untimely death if they presume their ability to win her over. And like the warrior Goddesses of every culture that are her sisters, she slays in an uncompromising manner.

Like Kali and to some extent Artemis, Durga symbolizes Time, the allure of youth, and the death of the ego through inevitable physical demise. However, her major role is that of active Justice. She works as an antidote to all that is pernicious to spiritual growth and well-being, usually represented by demons, or *Assuras* as they are known in Hindu lore.

The Priestess of Durga: The Warrior Woman and Exemplar of Female Strength

This character uses her femininity to the hilt and loves the illusion of vulnerability that it creates. She is as fair in her judgements as in her looks, but she will right injustices in a trice when the opportunity presents itself. Working with grace and skill, Durga dispatches the enemies of morally correct living into the next dimension. The priestess of Durga works on the same level psychologically.

Durga not only refuses to marry but also eats meat and drinks wine, both of which are taboo in traditional Hindu lore. Thus she and her priestess are considered to be rebels who pay little or no heed to convention, either social or religious. Of course, Durga is herself sacrosanct and can do no wrong, cosmically speaking. While the same may not be said of her priestess, it is true that if her convictions are solid and her motives morally upright, she cannot go wrong, however bellicose her medium. The keynotes to the priestess of Durga are beauty, grace, ferocity and rectitude.

Clearly this denotes a shock factor, so we may also conclude that the woman who works on this wavelength is unconventional, both naturally and deliberately, and merrily flouts the norm. Admittedly, the same could be said of many a priestess!

HATHOR

The Egyptian Goddess Hathor is the more earthy equivalent of Isis or Auset. While Auset is sky, Moon and sea, Hathor is Earth, Moon and hearth.

Representing celestial fecundity and nurturing, and wearing the crescent Moon on her brow, Hathor protects children, the pregnant and nursing, and presides over fertility and childbirth. She is similar to Laxmi in that good health and abundance are guaranteed when she is in one's life. She represents nourishment on every level.

However, Hathor is no walkover. In Egyptian myth, when angered she becomes Sekhmet, a bloodthirsty aspect of deity which can only be sated with revenge (in a just cause, of course) and stopped by alcohol. Indeed, the Gods get her so drunk on beer tinted red to look like blood that she falls asleep whilst avenging mankind's lack of respect for the Divine. Otherwise, she might have destroyed them. This certainly makes an interesting flip-side to the bovine-faced Goddess who represents nature and nurture.

Hathor is also known as 'Mother of Light' and in Egyptian myth she is credited with providing the souls of the deceased with the sustenance they required to exist after physical death. Thus her ministrations reach beyond the physical planes, and she provides the necessities that enable life to exist in a spiritual as well as bodily sense.

The Priestess of Hathor: She Who Sustains

The priestess of Hathor works as a comforter, a nurturer and a home-maker. She provides the basics, such as food, saturated in *prana*. She emanates warmth, largely because she knows that she too is loved. She wants to pass it on, and her means are practical.

This priestess is not a philosopher; she is practical by nature. She is, however, emotional and her wrath, when it occurs, is devastating. However, her emotional ties are so strong and generally so positive that she is forgiven in a trice once the storm has died down.

KALI

Kali is the destroyer of ego. With her many arms containing weapons she compassionately destroys the illusion of this reality. Only it doesn't feel compassionate at the time. It feels like living death.

The people who are on the edge, the people going nuts in the streets or in psychiatric wards, are all under the tender loving care of Goddess Kali. She is the patron saint of menstrual madness, the Queen of Chaos. It only appears to be chaotic because our sociological reality level is so very different from that of the Divine. But Kali is the Goddess who crashes the computers that are our brains. She presents a reality which flips the synapses out.

This blue/black-skinned deity is not kind to those who wish to live in the mundane world – now called the Kali Yuga for precisely this reason. Reality is breaking up under her blades. It always has been, for as long as we can remember. Arguably there were other places and epochs in which this was not the case – Atlantis, Lemuria and so on. But this era belongs to Kali, at least on certain wavelengths.

Kali encourages all that is taboo. She is the breaker-out from convention. Her priestesses are extreme, as indeed are her priests. They live on the edge. In her rituals, wine and other reality-changing substances are used to excess. Her name has several roots, but essentially it means 'Time'. This reflects the fact that time changes everything – including all that we desire and hold as normal. She is essentially evolution with its most terrifying face on.

Behind the mask of physicality there is an endless sea of bliss, striving and more bliss. That which seems indomitable, such as the flesh itself, becomes as nothing under the tutelage of Kali.

The emotions and spiritual insights inspired by Kali are mind-bending and never kind. However, behind the vicious veil, in which madness and destitution are inevitable, there exists the face of the Divine Mother. Kali in her other aspect is the embracer, the culler of sorrow. She is Death, in its best sense. Thank the Goddess for Death. We'd all be suffering eternally without it.

Kali also recycles us. She is cruel in that she gives birth to us and causes us to live in a particular part of her epoch, with its many personal drawbacks. She points out on a very personal level that all of us suffer in order to learn. But she is kind in that the suffering is finite, if we can only break through our ego lusts, give in to the compassion of the Divine and reflect it through ourselves. She is a true Goddess of duality, and the mundane world will seem vile and insane to those in the initial processes of her initiations. Afterwards, epiphany arrives, and it smells of flowers.

Then back we are sent for more of the same, until lessons are learned and we progress onto the next level of consciousness. In Hindu lore, this can be on other planets. The presence is not physical, of course. It is a very different wavelength from the one we inhabit and very difficult to access under normal states of consciousness. The moment we encounter evidence of the Kali Yuga, such as a street and block of houses made of concrete, or another person who is in a different frame of consciousness, a barrier can arise between us and the Divine. No wonder so many mystics are hermits.

However, to live in the midst of this life, with its numerous cross-references and the constant bombardments from sources alien to our personal ones (media, news, random people in the street, even friends and family), is also to be experiencing the initial stages of Kali-realization.

In their traditional Indian context Kali's initiates and neophytes meditate in cemeteries and perform extremely gruelling tasks of endurance. Some of the rituals of her divine husband, Siva, involve the digging-up and consuming of flesh and bones of their own ancestors.

We are perhaps fortunate not to have to go to such extremes in Western society in order to access the same wavelengths. We do not have to, as we have vivid accounts of lurid situations presented to us every day, either personally or through the media. Extreme personal challenges also present the same opportunity.

Living Hell is the ticket to Kali's incredible illuminations. So take heart if you are living in it. It's the ticket outward and upward.

The Priestess of Kali: She Who Terrifies

The archetypal priestess of Kali (as opposed to the orthodox Hindu) is deeply unconventional and will challenge on every level those with whom she interacts. She causes emotional and spiritual transformation, usually by rather unpleasant means. Full of sound and fury, but signifying everything, she will repulse many and attract the few who recognize the nature of the energy behind her actions.

This priestess is well aware that physical life is an illusion and that materialistic values lead nowhere. That is not to say that Kali's devotees do not crave wealth – of course they do, and many sacrifices have been made to the Goddess to this end. However, the priestess of Kali takes an overview of life and thus all physical matters are deemed ephemeral.

LAXMI

Laxmi is a Goddess of beauty and prosperity. Her aura is ghee-yellow and she glows from the inside like a candlelit altar viewed through a window. The window is of course our mundane reality.

Traditionally she is flanked by elephants, which represent her regal status, and golden coins flow from her upturned hands. Her presence brings life-sustenance, *prana*. She represents fertility, beneficence of all kinds and nurture. On a mundane level, she can bring money, or opportunities to gain it. Most importantly, however, she is the ever-kind, ever-blessing Goddess.

The gifts conferred by Laxmi include *kama*, 'supreme carnal pleasure', *moksa*, 'beauty', *dharma*, 'spiritual righteousness', and of course *artha*, 'wealth'. It goes without saying that Laxmi is one of the most popular deities in India, being a prime giver of life-enhancing boons. In many ways she performs the functions of a solar deity, bringing the conditions necessary for growth.

The Priestess of Laxmi: The Abundant One

This woman naturally sustains and nurtures – not simply family (indeed, often not), but friends and apparently random persons too. She brings a strong sense of safety in all senses. She is food, shelter and friendship. She also provides wealth and through that health on many levels.

MAAT

The Egyptian Goddess Maat represents solace and protection from injustice. With her impeccable ability to weigh and measure man's soul and motives, we may rely on her for consolation, the righting of wrongs and fairness. Her symbols are the scales and the feather, with which she measures the virtue of the dead. If their hearts are heavier than the feather, they are condemned. If, however, they balance or are lighter, the soul is free to progress into the underworld under the aegis of Osiris.

Maat is, however, also merciful. Punishment is waived if redeeming qualities are found. In the Negative Affirmation after death, one is interrogated as to whether one has stolen or committed adultery or other misdeeds during life. Even if one is found guilty on every count, Maat will waive punishment if the following question can be answered positively: Is there one person who is glad that you were born? Needless to say, this lets most people off the hook.

Maat essentially means 'Truth', which of course is a matter of perspective and open to debate. Ancient Egyptians were urged to 'Speak Maat, do Maat!', indicating that the qualities of this Goddess include a sense of social justice. To some extent she represents the acceptable norm. As a Goddess, however, her qualities are also sublime and spiritual.

The Priestess of Maat: The Peacekeeper

With a strong sense of liberty and justice, the priestess of Maat is the diplomat, the communicator between rival camps, the mediator.

Her sense of balance informs her every move. She is often involved in politics, but maintains an open mind in her mediations. She makes an excellent High Court judge or member of a jury.

The priestess of Maat is naturally fair and therefore ideally suited to situations which require a sense of objectivity. She understands the motives that inform the actions of others without being judgemental about their manifestation. I am reminded of Gill Edward's book *Stepping into the Magic (see Recommended Reading)*, in which she discusses the role of the deviant in society. As she sees it, this person is acting as a sort of psychic scapegoat for the rest of us, fulfilling a sub-conscious role which is necessary in the realms of duality.

Paramahansa Yogananda says something equivalent in his *Auto-biography of a Yogi (see Recommended Reading)*, when he discusses 'the movie-screen of God's mind'. He sees the many nightmarish aspects of life on Earth as spiritual illusions (that's not to deny their immediate effect on us or the 'victims') which occur in order to give us a greater sense of Cosmic Justice – and dualistic balance.

The philosophies behind this highly controversial standpoint are native to the priestess of Maat. She knows the pros and cons of every situation and is compassionate and cosmically balanced in her approach to all matters. It is her 'job' to keep the balance.

THE MUSES

The Muses are part of the retinue of Apollo. As well as representing the intellectual faculties, solar functions and the destruction of pestilence, Apollo is a God of music. As such, he is surrounded by nine lovely nymph-like ladies, each one representing a different creative talent. They are usually said to be the children of Zeus (as are most Greek Gods and Goddesses) and Mnemosyne ('Memory'). They work together as a chorus or choir, highlighting nine specific disciplines. Essentially, the Muses are nine priestesses of very specific skills.

Calliope represents epic poetry and the art of articulation, while her sister *Clio* is the Muse of history and, doubtlessly, its telling in epic verse. *Erato's* name gives away the area over which she presides, that of epic love poetry and erotic self-expression. *Euterpe* symbolizes the skills of flute-playing, while *Melpomene* presides over the great Greek art of tragedy. The latter performed a religious function, acting as catharsis for an entire culture. Rather than the individual performing acts of criminal deviance, the dark side of ancient Greek culture was vicariously sated, courtesy of Melpomene's dramaturgy.

In close association with this faculty is the Muse of mimic art, *Polyhymnia*. Their sister *Terpsichore* presides over lyric poetry and dance, both skills used in religious oration and ritual. *Thalia*, on the other hand, inspires divine laughter. She is the Muse of Comedy.

Finally we also have *Urania*, the Muse of astronomy. It is interesting to see astronomy, which nowadays is considered a science rather than an art, included in the retinue of inspiration and arts. It is not even astrology, the study and interpretation of constellations, planets and their effects, which is represented here, but the Patrick Moore-style astronomy. How far the 'disciplines' have now been separated! Indeed, I was once asked to interview the famous astronomer Patrick Moore for a Liverpool newspaper. I was told beforehand to be careful to use the right terminology, as he had hung up the phone on the last interviewer for referring to astrology rather than astronomy! Quite an understandable reaction on his part, but it is interesting to note that in ancient Greece the two subjects were intimately linked.

Originally, the intuitive and creative arts were considered to be divine representations and reflections, crafts of the priestess; there was no rift between these and what we would nowadays call the sciences.

Then the logos became associated with professionalism and masculinity, while the intuitive arts were derided as effete or unreliable because these were the skills of the priestess and the Old Religion was perceived as a threat to the new and was therefore divorced from the so-called 'respectable' arts such as astronomy. Admittedly it was not until the late Middle Ages that this dichotomy really took shape; as you will recall, the 'occult' arts used to be considered part of the Renaissance man's working portfolio. It was not until the establishment of the Church of England and the spawning of Catholic versus Protestant sentiment that the arts represented by the Muses really became defiled and separated.

As modern priestesses of every function – artistic, intuitive, logical and so-called 'scientific' – we aim to reunite the arts and vaunt the Goddess behind all aspects of human endeavour, as did the Muses themselves.

The Priestess of the Muses: The Source of Inspiration

Here the priestess acts as a direct conduit for the energy of Venus, the sphere from which all artistic inspirations emanate. Virtually every great creative man has had such a creature in his life, often a detached person who 'has a life' independent of their adorer. The Muse is not a typical partner or wife, and is often a lover only on the astral, propelling her admirer to great heights through unfulfilled desire, as Maud Gonne did for W. B. Yeats. She represents the Great Unobtainable and her energies can often be earthed by physical love.

The Muse is the archetypal priestess in that she inspires humanity to great creativity. She is often (though not always) physically very beautiful, in whatever form beauty may take in her era.

Elizabeth Siddal, for example, the wife of Dante Gabriel Rossetti, was the main Muse of the Pre-Raphaelite era. She appears in many of the paintings we cherish from that period. Ironically, her sittings for the famous painting 'Ophelia', during which she had to lie in a cold bath for hours on end, caused her early death by tuberculosis. During her marriage to the artist, she was unhappy because he found other Muses (mistresses) and no longer focused on her exclusively. Such is the nature of desire. After her death, he became obsessed again, burying his latest poems in her coffin. Seven years later, convinced that his 'best work' was buried with his one-time Muse, he had her exhumed in order to retrieve his precious tracts, only to find that they were far from as great as he had recalled.

Unless she can maintain her personal integrity throughout the intense exchange with her highly creative other, the Muse (or priestess of the Muses) is usually swapped for another in due course. Gala Dali managed to maintain her husband's obsession until her death by remaining in many ways (including perhaps sexually) aloof.

This priestess inspires sexual and intellectual desire and aspiration in one or more others. It is up to her to control this current by considering the loss to humanity if she becomes too intimately involved and earths the energy. Dion Fortune talks of this in her discussions of polarity in magickal workings. Her literary heroine and alter-ego Morgan Le Fay (in *The Sea Priestess* and *Moon Magic*) inspires intrigue and desire in the main character, Wilfred Maxwell, introduces him to Magick and ritual and then leaves him to get married to a 'nice girl' who will fulfil his human needs whilst leaving space for the Great Other – the priestess, the Goddess.

The Muse *provokes*. When the energy of untenable desire is at its peak, or getting there, intense Magick is possible. It becomes visionary due to many faculties being stimulated simultaneously. The Muse is often the unsung energy behind great art, literature and socio-political movements. Of course, she represents the Goddess, often in her cold aspect. See also Robert Graves' interaction with his wife Laura Riding – truly a terrifying and inspiring 'White Goddess'.

PERSEPHONE

Persephone's myth is one of the most important to the priestess. This basis of the Eleusinian Mysteries represents a spiritual and psychological cycle which is key to initiation. The tale is an agricultural allegory in which Demeter, the corn Goddess, goes into mourning when her daughter, initially known as Kore ('Maiden'), is abducted by the lord of the underworld. This part of the myth represents innocence lost. Kore is gathering flowers when her uncle Hades, knowing that she would never willingly become his bride, decides to open a chasm in the earth and swallow her into his subterranean kingdom.

Demeter is understandably grief-stricken by the loss of her daughter and withdraws her bounty from the world as a result. Mankind comes close to starvation. Hermes and Hecate help Demeter look for Kore, but she cannot be traced. Eventually she is discovered in Hades' kingdom, but he refuses to part with his enforced bride. Persephone meanwhile has eaten a pomegranate seed, which means that she can never wholly leave the underworld. In symbolic terms, this represents the seed of knowledge, which means that Persephone can never return to her 'maidenhood' or naïve original state. By entering the underworld, she has learned the secrets of the dead and has therefore been initiated into a powerful new state of being. She has become the High Priestess.

A compromise is finally reached: Persephone will return to her mother's domain for approximately a third of the year, representing

Spring and early Summer, but then she must return to Hades' baleful domain, representing Autumn and Winter. Demeter's 'cloak' – that is, the greenery of the Earth – alters according to her daughter's whereabouts.

Obviously this myth has many more permutations, but we can simplify them into two stages, those of the Mysteries of Eleusis. The first may be categorized as rites of purification. The Greater Mysteries are concerned with the act of transformation. In Persephone's myth, the effects of abduction and rape are sublimated into epiphany and rebirth. This powerful allegory therefore shows that both light and darkness are essential to the cosmic dynamic. Without them, growth would not be possible.

Another essential dynamic to the myth of Demeter and Persephone is of course the mother–daughter relationship. The Goddess Demeter represents all that is fecund and beneficent to life. She is the Greek equivalent of the Hindu Goddess Laxmi. One of Persephone's roles in this myth is to represent humanity itself, born and nurtured in trust, but then inevitably encountering divorce from the succouring life-force. This occurs naturally when we reach maturity and realize that the world is not a place of unconditional love, but rather one in which we are constantly challenged. Some of these challenges, being true initiations, take us to the depths of our own psyches and beyond, and the continued care of the mother becomes a matter of trust. Just as Persephone had to hope that she had not been forgotten by her loving parent and the other Gods, so every initiate has to trust that the Goddess is present as they enter the Dark Night of the Soul that is an initial stage in any meaningful spiritual process. Kali is another, much more violent representative of the same principles.

The Priestess of Persephone: The Fallen One

This priestess knows what she is from an early age, as she is prone to childhood psychism and usually has a rocky ride psychologically. Her mythological archetype is Persephone, abducted at an early age by her uncle Hades and forced to become wedlocked to Death. Through this abduction of her innocence, she becomes Queen of the Dead and keeper of all of their secrets. Her modern manifestation is magickally-minded, solemn and attracted to High Magick and ritual.

This visionary priestess is of course excellent at divination. She may be spontaneously telepathic, but she benefits greatly from the structure that Tarot cards and similar systems give to her visions. Likewise she operates well within hierarchical structures; indeed, of all priestess archetypes she is the ultimate adept at understanding sign and symbol and at cracking esoteric codes.

Her natural dignity makes her the ideal Goddess-representative in ritual Magick. She is a channel and blessed with excellent astral vision. Her suffering is translated into knowledge. In the myth, following her imprisonment Persephone becomes privy to the secrets of the dead. What she loses in liberty she gains in understanding. Thus the act of synthesis is one of the qualities of this priestess.

We could put it this way:

Cerebral priestess *(of Athene, Sarasvati, Maat, etc.)* = Thesis

Warrior priestess *(of Durga, the Morrigan, etc.)* = Antithesis

Visionary priestess *(of Perspehone, Auset, etc.)* = Synthesis

All three aspects are required to enable a spiritual and evolutionary dynamic to take place.

VENUS (APHRODITE)

Venus (Roman) or Aphrodite (Greek) was originally a Goddess of agricultural fecundity, as well as of human and animal fertility. In ancient Greece she became Aphrodite Urania, a sky Goddess of the same variety somewhat comparable to the Egyptian Nut. As a celestial deity, she is reflected here in her aspect as protector and initiatrix of pure Love.

This Goddess is, however, better known for her role as Aphrodite Porne (yes, really! The Greek word translates as 'courtesan'). She blesses and perpetuates sexual love ('venality' as it was known in regard to her Roman persona). She later became associated with the sea, from which she was alleged to have been born, her name being closely associated with the word 'foam'.

Most of us are well aware of the marine associations of Venus/Aphrodite, re-created in the fifteenth century by Botticelli, in whose iconic painting 'Birth of Venus' an angelic-looking Goddess floats gracefully to shore on a gigantic sea-shell. This is the legacy which has endured, and the symbols of this Goddess habitually accepted today revolve around her aquatic persona.

Venus/Aphrodite is of course one of the most popular Goddesses, as she enhances love and sex, causes ever-dear to the human heart. Because of this, she is still very much alive in Western society and is often consciously invoked by women (and men) preparing themselves for potential partnership. The sensual aspect is obvious: luxurious scented bubble baths, the combing of hair and general grooming, and the application of make-up to create glamour.

See the next chapter for some tips and descriptions of this most pleasurable of priestess paths. Virtually every woman becomes a priestess of Venus at least once in her lifetime.

WHICH PRIESTESS ARE YOU?

In the meantime, if you are unsure as to which deities to work with, why not try the quiz below? As well as helping you to deduce which Goddess or priestess path you most belong to at any given time, if you work in a group, it could help you deduce which roles should be played by which person at this particular point.

This is designed to be fun rather than life-defining. You may find that the archetype changes from one week to the next. This is quite normal, as we all go through many shades of pale or dark in a week. Most of us are unique combinations of traits, and of course mundane circumstances affect one's psychology. One of the most important qualities of the priestess is versatility, and this may be reflected in the answers you receive.

Simply answer the following questions and then count up the letters you tick, see which you have most of and read the relevant answer at the end. If you have an equal number, read all the relevant answers and select a deity whose properties include some of the traits of each.

1. *What is your current mood or general stance?*
    a) Happy
    b) Peaceful
    c) Depressed/melancholy
    d) Angry
    e) Adventurous

2. *How do you interact with most others at present? Are you:*
    a) Outgoing
    b) Nurturing
    c) Introvert

d) Passionate

e) Challenging

3. *How would you define your permanent temperament?*
   a) Highly variable
   b) Emotional/sentimental
   c) Creative
   d) Volatile
   e) Just/balanced

4. *What kind of role do you think you play in the main?*
   a) Friend or equal
   b) Family member
   c) Innovator
   d) Protector
   e) Academic

5. *How would you define your current lifestyle?*
   a) Adventurous
   b) Homely
   c) Retired
   d) Career-orientated
   e) Aspirational/transformative

6. *What are your future aspirations?*
   a) Don't know yet
   b) Family home
   c) Self-renewal/significant change of lifestyle
   d) Social/political advancement
   e) Travelling

7. *How would you define your love life at present?*
   a) Experimental
   b) Steady
   c) Happy on your own
   d) Explosive
   e) Still trying

8. *What kind of domestic life do you lead?*
   a) Being looked after by parents/other
   b) Homemaker
   c) Secure
   d) Erratic
   e) Independent

9. *Physically speaking, would you describe yourself as:*
   a) Erratic
   b) Comfortable
   c) Challenged
   d) Athletic
   e) Lazy

10. *What is your ideal form of work or career?*
    a) Student
    b) Domestic
    c) Institutional
    d) Artistic/creative
    e) Political/social mover and shaker

11. *How would you define your spiritual inclinations?*
    a) Undecided

b) Developing
c) Orthodox
d) Devoted
e) Cynical

Answers

As mentioned above, it is usual for us to be a mixture of many arche-types and moods, which is why you may have found some of the answers difficult to define. However, this quiz gives the *general* arche-type to which you most relate at this time.

Mostly As: The Virgin/Maiden

The archetype to which you are most affiliated at present is that of the Virgin, or Maiden Goddess. The deities ascribed to this archetype include Artemis, Selene and Persephone. Your qualities include independence, an explorative nature and a visionary aspect. This means that you are likely to undergo dramatic transformations over the next few years and will not remain static in the personality which others know you by now. You will achieve this by striving to follow your goals. You are an ever-changing soul who is on the up, challenging though circumstances will certainly be.

Try to maintain your sense of fun and adventure. Even though you will go through times which are deeply discouraging, as we all do, you have the potential to become visionary, self-defining and to act as a High Priestess. Keys to this include meditating on the Moon and study-ing the arts of sign and symbol, that is to say esoteric lore.

Divination is a path to self-realization. If you have received mostly As, you are encouraged to explore it. This can be via the Tarot, runes, skrying or any other means *(see pages 73–81)*. Pick the one that feels best to you.

Mostly *Bs*: The Mother

You are the provider, the channel of divine beneficence. Your role may appear mundane on the outside, but you are actually performing a task essential to humankind. If you focus on this task, you will find other things happening to you later that relate more to your personal development. You are on hold at the moment, but later in life you will find your niche spiritually and personally.

Your main deities include Hathor, Demeter and Laxmi. Hathor, with her cow's head and human body, represents cosmic milk and thus sustenance. Demeter is Goddess of the corn, on whose bounty humankind relies for survival. Laxmi is a Goddess of prosperity, health and nurture. The mother archetype is a priestess of these deities, amongst others.

Playing a conventional, familiar role is a path to self-realization at this point in your incarnation.

Mostly *Cs*: The Crone

You relate at present to the Crone aspect of the Goddess. She is wise, world-weary, but upbeat in her own unique way. The Goddesses which relate to this state of mind include Hecate of Greek lore and Vidya Bagala of Hindu philosophy. The latter symbolizes knowledge obtained through negativity from others, the type of psychic fallout that we all experience from time to time in our day-to-day lives. This is a case of 'suffer to learn'.

As the Crone, you are the transmitter of knowledge and experience. Having been on the 'inside', you now possess objectivity. You have passed your tests with honours – a fact well worth remembering when you are tempted to despair that the best is behind you. In fact, it is the worst that is past and you have now attained a plateau from which to consider your next move.

Your path to self-realization is steady, measured retrospection and the transformation of knowledge into a format accessible to others.

Mostly Ds: The Warrior/Sorceress

You are a warrior priestess. This means that you fight for what you believe in and are always adept at counteracting the energies that you believe to be negative. You are a true priestess of the unconventional – which any priestess always is. You might occasionally consider yourself weak, but this is because you are fighting demons every day, and I do not simply mean in the Buffy sense. You are a groundbreaking priestess: congratulations!

Because of your talent for innovation, you also look at 'alternative' means to achieve your goals. This capacity allies you with magickal archetypes such as the Celtic sorceress Cerridwen and the Greek Circe.

Other major deities include the Hindu demon-slayers Durga and Kali. Difficult, but enjoy them! They offer many rewards after their battles have taken place.

Your path to self-realization is to fight for a just cause, to allow yourself free expression, including when it defies convention, and to meet all challenges with enthusiasm.

Mostly Es: The Peacekeeper

You are one of the most balanced and measured priestess archetypes. You have an intellectual and fair overview of the situations you encounter. The Goddesses to whom you are allied include Maat, Athene and Sarasvati.

Like Maat, you will judge situations and people with an objectivity tinted only by compassion. Your essential nature is redemptive.

Like Athene, you have strong cerebral and intellectual leanings. Through Sarasvati, these find creative expression; Sarasvati presides over poetry, music and academic pursuit. Pens are sacred to her in India, thus she is also Goddess of scribes and artists. As priestess of these and lateral deities, you are in a good position to analyse, reflect and create.

Though you will at times doubt yourself, as any sane priestess does, you can rely on your intuition and common sense to bring you through. Just keep on keeping on. It will bring its dividends in the end.

Your path to self-realization is to work within a conventional structure whilst purveying ideas and concepts which are pure and honourable, and thus not necessarily usual in this context. You will also find analysis and artistic expression of your thoughts and feelings to be of great personal value.

The Everyday Priestess

This book is about all aspects of being a priestess. This includes physical health, beauty and self-expression. Dion Fortune's sea priestess and heroine, Morgan Le Fay, is incredibly 'well-preserved', uses unguents to keep her skin youthful and uses her looks to attract and hold the magnetism of her priests. Charisma is the real name of the game, of course, but the priestess has the perfect opportunity and excuse to enjoy her physical body.

It should be obvious that we are not just talking about conventional or external beauty here. Health, beauty and Magick all come from within, and the most enchanting characteristic in the world is confidence.

All of us have features we are not 100 per cent happy with. Few people consider themselves to be beautiful; we are taught that thinking so is vain, and anyway, we are usually too busy focusing on our imperfections to enjoy our good points. The fact is, aesthetics are thoroughly a matter of opinion. Some of our inclination is simple chemistry; some is learned response. Size, shape and vital statistics of any sort can be beautiful; it all depends on the person who's carrying them. So this Venusian chapter is about attitude too.

The priestess uses what the Goddess has given her to the best advantage. Sometimes she wishes to pass unnoticed, and this is ideal for many mundane situations. However, when she wishes to scintillate and shine, when she wishes to use her inner Magick, she does so with aplomb.

Whatever the scenario, character and mood can have an effect which entirely changes the physical appearance, or at least the perception of it, and under the control of a feisty and magickally-minded individual, any body becomes beautiful. How so? By focusing the attentions of the observer on your wonderful, unique and magickal personality! Working with Goddesses tends to rub off in this way too, investing the priestess with extra glamour and mystique – that certain *je ne sais quoi* to which charm is often attributed. The Golden Dawn priestesses *(see Chapter 2)* had the arts of self-presentation off to a tee.

All of us are beautiful and unique. Learning to love your own image is tantamount to accepting with grace your role in the world. Therefore we will also be looking at how to feel at home in the body and how to love our physical idiosyncrasies. There is nothing wrong with striving towards one's optimum physical potential, even if its manifestation may seem superficial compared to the other qualities of the priestess. Each and every one of us is capable of extraordinary beauty, inside and out; and there is nothing wrong with having a little fun along the way.

So here we will explore how to improve whatever the Goddess has given you, how to enjoy an enchanted life (or evening) whatever your dress-size or how conventionally attractive you may be, and how to permeate your physical appearance with the true beauty of Magick. The fact that this will make you look a million times better too is, well, a happy side-effect.

MAGICK MIRROR

This fun technique is based on aspects of Witchcraft and creative visualization.

- *Buy yourself a beautifully decorated mirror, preferably one with a handle. On a night of a Waxing Moon, hold it in the moonlight and view yourself through it, saying:*

  > *Mirror cast in moonlight bright,*
  > *Make me fairer by thy light.*
  > *Help me love my earthly face,*
  > *And fill my soul with power and grace.*
  > *When I view myself in thee,*
  > *This is how I Will to Be.*

  or a similar chant or affirmation. These childlike verses may seem rather gauche, but they work because of their very simplicity.

- *This is the most important part, however: when you look into your Magick Mirror, always make sure you are visualizing yourself as you wish to become. This is not always possible with normal mirrors, which may give us a nasty shock when we glance into them at an unflattering moment! You have control of your Magickal Reflection, however, and can work on continually improving your gorgeous image in it.*

- *If you have a particular physical blemish, when you look into your Magick Mirror, envisage yourself without it. Also picture yourself full of confidence and glowing with health and scintillating energy. Use it whenever you are making physical improvements to your face and for all of your beauty spells and enchantments.*

You will notice that your self-image, and perhaps even the way you look, varies depending on your context and the people who surround you. A classic example is that when admiration and flirtation are encountered, the recipient almost always glows aurically, and their features are physically as well as psychically enhanced. This is because we all thrive on positive energy. Similarly, if one is surrounded by younger, trendier, more confident people, the self-image can crash, and with it, one's aura of beauty.

It is worth experimenting with this and trying to maintain confidence whatever the context. If we can carry our auric glow with us at all times, the qualities of our particular character and looks will be appreciated whoever surrounds us.

THE POWER OF CLOTHES

When I was at the Witchcraft Seminars in Cornwall recently, I was delighted to find that we were treated to a fashion show – literally, what the well-dressed witch is wearing this season! And why not? Right in the middle of lectures on stone circles, the Sabbats, spell-casting and a variety of other 'serious' topics, we were treated to the 'fun' aspect of magickal glamour.

Wonderful clothes enhance our confidence as well as appearance; they are mystical magickal robes even when they appear to be reasonably normal. The colour and texture of our garments affect us all day, sitting straight on the skin, and their style can completely affect our mood – business-like or sexy, sporty or mystical. Personally I love gothic-style clothes, with their dark sweeping velvets and ribbons and luscious textures, but I wouldn't pop to the supermarket in them unless I actually wanted to attract unwanted attention.

Clothes are also a case of context and self-definition, a fun way to make any body look good – whatever one's size, shape and height. If we can develop sartorial flair, we're well on our way to looking and feeling magickal all day long.

The colour, texture and style of clothes are key points to anyone. However, the priestess has other issues to consider too. When we pull on our jeans or slip into that black pvc dress, we associate ourselves with a certain group mind. This operates in two ways: how we are perceived by others and how we perceive ourselves.

If we go around looking as if we live in a squat or a hovel, people will respond accordingly, with whatever preconceptions their experience has led them to. I went through a very punky stage when I was younger and used to get followed around shops by suspicious assistants, much to my annoyance. I even began to feel guilty by association, which demonstrates the ways in which this 'group mind' can impinge on our moods.

Similarly, wearing lovely clothes which look expensive (even if they're not) will make people perceive you as 'decent' and well-to-do (especially if you look refreshed and have a confident air), and treat you accordingly. Ridiculous but true.

This simple psychology has the bonus of allowing us to play with images and moods and to manipulate the group mind too. Every punk, goth and outré dresser knows this. Look at Zandra Rhodes, with her fabulous colour-concoctions and amazing clothes – she exudes creativity and is a living advertisement for her own designs. In contrast we have chic, sleek Isabella Blow, whose sharp bob and à la mode hats convey the instant message of sophistication and wealth. Fashion icons specialize in the manipulation of the group mind, and as we visualize ourselves, so we become. Clothes can be the external expression of this self-image, and sometimes the living proof. It is easy to dress magickally – that is, in a way that will positively enhance our own mood and the way we are perceived by others.

The texture of one's garments has an immediate effect on the aura. Some synthetic materials can cause energy blockages, which is why magickal robes are best made out of natural cotton. Silk, on the other hand, is luxuriant and positive against the skin, although it has the side-effect of insulating the aura. Thus silk is good for those feeling psychically or psychologically attacked – working with hostile associates, for example. Tarot cards are kept wrapped in silk for the same reason – their magickal aura is preserved from outside influences. One of my friends, a practitioner of Chinese medicine in the City, wears wool to insulate himself from the constant bombardment of negative or intrusive vibrations encountered on the Tube or in the office. He reckons that it's worth undergoing the extra warmth, even on hot days!

It is usually best to avoid man-made materials, although this is not of course always possible. Always read the labels before you buy clothes – it is surprising how many synthetics are used with natural fibres. For magickal work and meditation, stick to the all-natural.

Velvets are flattering on practically everyone, whether voluminous or tight (basques, for example), and they truly absorb magickal atmospheres, making them a suitable alternative to cotton in ritual wear.

Materials such as denim, however, have the opposite effect – they ground and externalize energy. Practical, yes, but not particularly enchanting. Nobody looks or feels truly magickal in a pair of ordinary jeans. A pair of light *flared* denims, on the other hand, conveys a sense of style as well as making the leg look long and thin, and purple-tinted denim changes its vibe altogether. The idea of creativity is conveyed by the slight alteration in style and colour, and the group perception shifts accordingly. A while ago I bought three pairs of identical flared denin jeans. One of these I soaked overnight in purple Dylon. They came out just a few shades more vibrant than the blue jeans, but the impact was entirely different. Adding personal touches to one's attire will make a world of magickal difference.

Colour also has an immediate effect on the aura:

Pale Pink: Conveys vulnerability, gentleness, femininity. Gives the impression of innocence.

Pale Blue: Calming, meditative. A colour which will attract virtually no attention, so good for those days when you want to keep yourself to yourself.

Navy Blue: A 'sensible' and grounding colour, good for just getting on with a job in hand. This colour will make people perceive you as reliable.

Purple: The most spiritual of colours, which cannot help but attract magickal energies into your day. Indigos will have a subtly different effect from dark purples, which convey a more solemn atmosphere. Good for astral connections and perceptions.

Sunshine Yellow or Orange: Gives the impression of absolute confidence – probably because it takes it to wear such a bright colour! Will attract attention and is not recommended for magickal work (unless you're assuming the form of a solar deity of course!), though it will enhance your mood at social events.

Pale Yellow: Gives a soft, child-like aura. Gentle and feminine.

Emerald Green: Conveys vibrancy and an atmosphere of natural Magick.

Black: The best of all colours for the magickally-minded. Black covers us with the cloak of Nuit, the Egyptian Goddess whose body is the night sky. It insulates the aura without stifling it. It gives confidence and psychic protection. A very sexy colour too, and flattering to all shapes and sizes.

White: Conveys the illusion of wealth – possibly because it's so difficult to keep white clothes perfect. Naturally, white has associations with spiritual cleanliness. White ritual robes suggest lustral rites and purification.

Red: A power colour! Wear red to feel sexy and confident. In winter, red clothes will make you feel warmer through their association with the element of Fire.

So, the clothes we wear can be included in our metaphysical outlook and become a fun way of both expressing ourselves and affecting others. They can of course be used in enchantments and spells to create very specific results. Here are a few examples:

○ *If you have a special occasion coming up, take one (or all) of the garments you intend to wear. Select a gemstone (or several) which gives the properties you desire - rose quartz for a successful date, for example, quartz crystal for insight, tiger's eye for confidence. Soak them in a bowl of water overnight. Assuming that your clothes are handwashable, place them in the empowered water and then let them dry naturally.*

- ○ *Cast a spell directly on your item of clothing. This can be done in any number of ways. You might like to see your Magick being absorbed into the fibres, or you could direct it into a piece of jewellery you will wear with the outfit. You could sew a magickal sigil or just a stitch of empowered thread into the garment. Clothes are great for magickal purposes as they interact directly with the aura and there are plenty of places in them to hide secret charms.*

- ○ *Soak your item of clothing in a magickally-charged oil. Be careful, however, not to get blotches of oil on your outfit. I like to use lavender, jasmine and rose oils as soaks for my clothes, or patchouli. The scent permeates the fibres and lasts longer. It also increases with body-heat, which can be nice if you're out for a long night on the tiles; perfume applied directly to the skin gives off more immediate scent, but it fades more quickly.*

- ○ *Have fun with your image! And always visualize yourself as quietly stunning (no need to be overboard about it; a very off-putting trait). Bear in mind that you are beautiful and unique, and exactly where you are meant to be on your magickal, mystical journey through life. So enjoy yourself! This is the best spell of all, and you will be extra-charming as a result.*

EYE MAKE-UP

Make-up is very effective for ritual. It sends subconscious signals to those around us, a trait observable in nature everywhere. These symbols can indicate danger, sex or illusion (camouflage, for example, or extra eyes on wings or plumage). It is potent stuff even in the so-called 'civilized' world. Many women look better without make-up, but using it can be fun, and effective in ritual. Many of the world's most effective priestesses use it to its optimum potential whilst representing the Goddess.

Eyes are the most important feature. Think of the way the sublimely beautiful Hindu and Egyptian Goddesses are portrayed, with their abundant dark eyeshadow and eyeliner tapering out to the side of the face to make the eyes look bigger, even from the side. Kohl is one of the most magickal beauty products and was used lavishly by the Ancient Egyptians.

Many spirituality-orientated beauty tips can be found in Catherine Wishart's book *Teen Goddess: How to Look, Love and Live Like a Goddess* (it's not just for teens, though!). She gives ideas for mixing make-up with ritual – a powerful technique used by shamans and priestesses for thousands of years – and makeovers relating to particular Goddesses.

Here is one example of a magickal makeover for any occasion:

 ### How to Give Yourself the Gaze of a Goddess

You will need:

❂ *Your Magick Mirror*

❂ *A black kohl eyeliner pencil*

❂ *A black liquid eyeliner*

☼ Metallic or black eyeshadow - use a shade that suits. I prefer purples and blacks to go with my own eyes, but it all depends on the shade of your iris and your hair colour. The best type of applicator is the simple sponge-tipped type. Always make sure it is clean when you use it.

☼ A decent black mascara

☼ Light eyeshadow

● Use the black kohl pencil to draw a line on the lower rim of each eye. Though this look became unfashionable for a while as people were squeamish about applying the pencil there, it is by far the most effective way of highlighting the eye and gives a wonderful vampish effect too. Be gentle, of course.

● Using the sponge-tipped applicator, apply the eyeshadow to the place just above your eyelid - essentially, follow the shape of your eye socket. Although you will in no way end up looking like a panda, that is the shape we are aiming for.

● Take the liquid eyeliner and paint a straight even line from about half an inch from the outer corner of the eye to the inner corner by the bridge of the nose. Needless to say, this takes a steady hand. Keep the line as thin, straight and close to your lashes as possible.

● Use the light eyeshadow to subtly emphasize the soft skin beneath the eyebrow. Smudge a little onto your eyelid and bleed it upwards to merge into your dark shadow. Apply your mascara.

● This look mixes best with dark lipstick.

● The Goddesses particularly apt to this image include Isis and Kali.

This is just one of many possible ideas – obviously different looks suit different people. Have some fun experimenting!

ENCHANTING HAIR

A person's crowning glory should not be underestimated magickally. Hair is one of the most potent magickal substances, along with nails and blood, as it contains a direct link to the person who grew it. Never let you hair fall into the wrong witch's hands – they could control you like a puppet with the hair to add to their spell!

On a cheerier note, hair can be used in all sorts of positive beauty-enhancing spells. Brushing your hair by moonlight in your Magick Mirror is a powerful process itself, especially when accompanied by a chant or attraction or glamour spell.

Oils are great for containing magickal vibrations, so why not enchant some olive or coconut oil and brush it into your locks? You can gear this to any purpose – just focus your intent on the oil placed on your altar or in the centre of your Circle, then brush it into your hair with a chant or simple rhyme that befits your intention. This is best done at night so that it can soak your strands with lustrous moisture and you can wash out the surplus the next day.

Hair holds scents for longer than other parts of the body, so adding magickal oils and perfumes to it will give you an enchanted aroma all night long. Musks and 'dark' scents like patchouli give a wonderful sensuality to the aura.

Another substance which is good for both hair and skin is the avocado. It contains vitamins A, C and E, all of which are essential for healthy skin and shiny hair, plus iron, potassium, niacin and other skin-nourishing goodies. Mixed with olive oil, egg white and a small banana (yes, really!), it makes a fantastic hair-and-face pack. It is especially important to treat your hair and face with vitamins C and E if you smoke. Smoking destroys these vitamins, which are needed to keep the face from sagging, hence the associations of smoking with premature ageing.

Hair is power. No matter what your facial shape or features, a great hairstyle, cut and colour will make a world of difference to the way you look and feel. Most of us are unable to radically change our facial features, but we *can* experiment with hair length and colour. You can use your hair colour in the same way you do your clothes – to suit every mood! Even if your hair is extremely dark, it can be given a wonderful red sheen by using a henna shampoo, for example, and 'hair mascaras' are available to streak your hair with highlights and zap it with cosmic glitter. Think Magick with the way you wear your crowning glory! And remember that hairstyles go a long way to affecting the way we are perceived. They help define your archetype.

Many magickally-inclined women and men wear their hair either long or in a mediaeval or Cleopatra-style bob. Both styles have mystical connotations and are 'timeless', unlike the ephemeral styles one gets at 'trendy' hairdressers. Some of these can look wonderful, though – it all depends on the cerebral atmosphere you're happiest with. Dreadlocks and beads and plaits and ribbons are also popular in magickal circles – as are hair-feathers!

It is easy to weave a spell or intent into your hair by plaiting it in (one lock is fine) whilst reciting something like the Witch's Ladder, as improvised below:

> *By plait of one, the spell's begun.*
> *By plait of two, it cometh true.*
> *By plait of three, So mote it Be,*
> *By plait of four, my Will is Law,*

By plait of five, the spell's alive,
By plait of six, my Will is fixed,
By plait of seven, in Earth and Heaven,
By plait of eight, my Will is Fate,
By plait of nine, the thing is mine!

The key point, as ever, is to imagine and will the thing you want at the same time as plaiting your hair and chanting the spell.

Adding Lustre to Your Locks

Shiny hair looks great on everyone, but the trick is to get the shine without the grease. Several shampoos contain amino acids, proteins and lecithin, all of which help increase gloss. For light, fine hair, wheat proteins work best, while amino acids and lecithin work best on darker, thicker hair. Olive and coconut oil work wonders on coarse hair. Olive oil has a long history of use in Magick, particularly in Greece. Coconut oil carries a different, more African vibration (thus relating to a different mythos). These oils can be brushed through and left for as long as is convenient to you; they help de-tangle too.

Little rituals such as hair treatments are great preliminaries to positive body-imaging and workings for love, lust and creativity. Remember to use that Magick Mirror!

HANDS

A priestess or witch's hands are magickal tools, doubling up as wands, chalices and swords (for casting Circles or invoking the Quarters) when no props present. Hands are also used to gesture and define, and as tools of communication via the creative processes of writing and artwork. In Hinduism and Buddhism, they are used to perform *Mudras*, meditative gestures attuned to specific energies. As such, they deserve our attention.

Jewellery is a wonderful enhancement to any priestess's closet, and a ring of significance looks lovely as well as carries special associations. Rings are intimate and they come with us everywhere. I have an emerald ring for constant rejuvenation and fresh energy, an Eye of Horus to remind me of the Eternal Spirit and a moonstone which I wear all the time. All of my jewellery is silver, as I adore the magickal, lunar associations and vibrations that come from this metal. Pick yours according to your own needs and associations and try not to wear random pieces of jewellery which aren't really 'you', as can happen when we receive gifts. It's better by far to wear jewellery which actually means something to *you* and which feels 'right'.

Since hands are such magickal objects – even containing our futures and pasts in their palms! – they deserve to be kept moisturized with fragrant oils and lotions, and sparkling with wonderful magickal energies. At the risk of sounding terribly mundane, be sure to wear rubber gloves when washing up, cleaning and gardening, or your travails will soon show.

And don't forget your nails. Long ones varnished with a colour of significance – silver, purple, whatever you fancy – really add to the glamour.

How to Give Yourself Magical Hands

You will need:

⊙ A tablespoon of neutral (unscented) moisturizer

⊙ A teaspoon of olive oil

⊙ A bottle of essential rose oil and one of jasmine (diluted is fine for the latter, which is very expensive bought neat!)

⊙ A bottle of purple or silver nail varnish, or a glitter mix

⊙ A stick of incense; lavender, rose or jasmine are particularly good

● Remove any nail varnish you are wearing and begin by washing your hands in warm water with soap and scrubbing under your nails. Dry your hands and give yourself a manicure if necessary – or even better, get somebody else to do it for you!

● Now take the oils and put five drops of each in with the moisturizer and mix them together. Imagine the mixture absolutely glowing with the energies of creativity.

● Put it to one side for a moment and carefully paint your nails. As you do so, think of all the reasons why you love every part of your body, but especially your hands and fingers.

● When your nails are thoroughly dry, treat your hands to the mixture. As you rub it in, imagine bursts of sparkling energy glimmering all over your hands and creativity swirling from them.

- Light the incense and pass your hands through the smoke, saying:

> Hands of Light,
> Hands of Fire,
> Hands which heal and which inspire.
> Hands of Air,
> Hands so Bright,
> Filled with Magick day and night.
> Hands create, Hands of Earth,
> Bring my astral dreams to birth.

This is a good preliminary ritual to an important creative act, such as sitting down to paint, write or make music.

SOME GENERAL TIPS

○ Use a face-splash of water in which a quartz crystal and/or rose quartz has been placed. As you splash your face with the water, be sure to visualize yourself in flawless form.

○ Visualize yourself constantly as a God/Goddess with beauty coming from the inside, whatever the outside might be undergoing. Use your Magick Mirror to affirm your beauty on all levels. Don't be discouraged - your skin will respond to this programming if you keep at it!

○ Exercise regularly outside. Make sure you build up a sweat when so doing. This cleans out toxins and gives the skin a fantastic natural glow.

☉ There has been much paranoia about sunlight over recent years, but studies prove that the skin (and soul!) require daily exposure to natural sunlight daily in order to produce vitamin D and essential serotonin – the chemical that makes us happy. So a brisk daily walk in the great outdoors is the very least we can do to keep our skins clear and our spirits up.

☉ Olive oil is a fantastic magickal oil (as is the lighter grapeseed) and can be used as a base for many lotions and potions. Essential oils mix beautifully in it and can be applied in conjunction with visualizations, spells and chants. Olive oil has the additional advantage of protecting the skin from some of the harmful effects of the sun.

☉ You can easily concoct gorgeous body lotions and scrubs by mixing and matching olive or grape oils with suitable essential oils. Ground avocado stones make a great exfoliator to add to a body-wash, and mashed fruit such as banana, avocado and strawberries work wonders for tired skin that's been exposed to too many pollutants (especially good for city-slicking priestesses!).

☉ Have regular magickal baths. These give a feeling of physical as well as auric well-being.

Here's just one example of a full magickal beauty regime:

- *Perform your chosen physical exercises and creative visualizations (see Chapter 3).*

- *Fetch (or prepare earlier) a glass of cider vinegar. This is an astringent and doesn't smell as bad as it sounds! Add to it several drops of rose oil, the same of jojoba and the same of geranium.*

- *Start running a bath and tip the mixture into the warm running water. When your bath is ready, add a handful of rose petals if possible. Have your Magick Mirror to hand. It is always preferable to bathe by candlelight and, if you fancy it, have a glass of something sparking on the side. After exercise, carbonated spring water is the best choice for this.*

- *Get into the bath and perform any visualizations or psychic attunements that are relevant to your work, or just kick back and let yourself dream.*

- *When you are ready, get out and splash your face with cold water to close the pores. Rub yourself down with a towel and put on a comfortable gown and play some soothing music.*

- *Moisturize your entire body with one of the potions mentioned in this book, or one of your own, and perform whichever of the above beauty treatments appeals to you.*

- *When you have finished, look in your Magick Mirror and thank the Goddess for the gift of your body.*

THE PRIESTESS AND SENSUALITY

The priestess uses sexual attraction to create an astral dynamic. This dynamic can be used for many purposes, such as physical/mental healing (the two are deeply linked), energy sharing and personal progression. We all know that the best feeling in the world is that of being in love – or in lust. The trick is not to dissipate the energy too fast, or possibly at all.

If the priestess decides to expend her energy in the physical sense, she will do it with skill, ideally at least. The subject of Tantra is way too vast to go into here, but it offers a selection of techniques whereby different energies and Magick may be channelled. However, the means do not necessarily have to be classically Tantric.

The ideal priestess is sensual without giving her energy away through emotional need. A philosophical overview is required. This is of course much easier said than done and most of us require a few serious learning experiences before we hit that point of realization. I know I did.

The priestess is, however, able to interact sexually if she desires, without guilt or inhibition. Again, this is a tough one for many of us! Even the amazing Golden Dawn priestesses had problems with that (one might say, especially so), but they came from a much more repressive era. That said, Aleister Crowley's priestesses of the same era seem to have taken a very different view of the subject. Sometimes, however, he was keener to work with prostitutes, as they were utterly impartial (I suspect the mage encountered a lack of magnetism, however), but in some ways they were performing the role of the classic priestess. They were vessels of a higher consciousness (no, I don't mean Crowley's!), as he was utilizing the intensity of the sexual interaction to focus his thoughts on various deities and to mediate through them the manifestation of his Higher Will, which included the rapid evolution and redemption of humanity.

Sensuality and sexuality are definitely of enormous use in Magick. It is certainly possible, and sometimes preferable, to work with those to whom no attraction is felt – this results in a more algebraic wavelength, more Yellow Ray or intellectual and generally compassionate. However, in much of the work of the priestess, a certain attraction is preferable, as it provokes a stronger response and has a chemical effect on the participant(s). This does not have to result in Bacchanalia, though in some rituals it may well do. The point is that the priestess is the provoker and recipient of spiritual, psychological and sometimes physical passion.

So enjoy yourself. And walk with the Goddess fixed in your inner vision.

Here is a simple technique to help you to feel like a love Goddess:

 ## Rose Oil Sensuality Bath

Bathing is one of the Goddess's gifts to women – it is both relaxing and entrancing. Ideas flow easily in the bath and beauty flourishes. The bathtub is a truly magickal place.

● *Baths are sacred to Venus/Aphrodite and reminiscent of her rising from the sea-foam in later Greek myth. Roses are also sacred to Venus/Aphrodite and have long symbolized beauty at its most gentle and feminine. Of course, with the symbolism of the thorny stalk included, the rose represents beauty protected, innocence guarded. The soft scent of the rose has become equated with the theme of youth and so roses are also symbolic keys to the secret of eternal youth. Their oil, petals and scent may be used to tap into this wavelength.*

- *Various gemstones can be left to soak in bathwater in order to invest it with their properties – for a Venusian bath, rose quartz is an obvious choice. Large hunks are easier to retrieve afterwards. It's always best to remove the gemstones before you get in.*

- *I often take ritual baths, for auric cleansing and psychological preparation. The tub is an ideal place in which to dream and creatively visualize. So pour yourself a glass of sparkling wine or a beverage of your choice, run a bath and be generous with the rose, ylang ylang and geranium oils.*

- *Whilst in soak, visualize yourself looking and feeling like a Love Goddess. Don't forget to visualize your body the way you intend it to become – rejuvenated, slim, healthy, curvier, or whatever your particular preferences may be.*

- *No matter what one's age, the body is always renewing its cells and it is never, never too late to rejuvenate and to feel sensual. This bathing/visualizing is a simple technique which many of us do naturally. And it works!*

SPELLS AND CHARMS FOR YOUTH AND BEAUTY

For I am the gate to eternal youth, the Cauldron of Cerridwen that is the Holy Grail of Immortality.

These words, taken from 'The Charge of the Goddess', reflect the intimate connection between regeneration (as opposed to youth) and Magick. Magick is a live current, like electricity, which has the power to enliven, quicken the senses and affect the body on every level.

Spiritually and psychologically, it keeps us full of potential. It causes us to become conduits of positive universal currents and prevents us from stagnating, either mentally or physically. If we are constantly attuned to the magickal realms, we will always carry a sense of child-like wonder and fun which in itself is a major ingredient for youthfulness. Cynicism is the death of beauty on many levels.

To keep yourself ever-youthful and magickal, try any (or all) of the following techniques.

Keep a Rose Quartz and/or Emerald about your Person

When you are feeling happy, imagine your positive emotions flowing into the stone and being locked there. Whenever you are feeling unhappy or lacking in energy, tap into the vibrations you have stored in your gemstones.

Emerald and rose quartz are especially good for locking in love energies. So a perfect time to lock up that energy for later use is at the beginning of a love affair, when you are excited and happy and charmed. Indeed, if more of us did this at the beginning of our relationships, there would be far less trauma to undergo at the end of them. For these stones and energies are ideal for healing purposes, especially broken hearts. And most of us know that a broken heart ages one like nothing else on Earth.

Generate Feelings of Love around Yourself

You can do this for yourself – you do not need to receive it from others. Love given is unfortunately often corrupt, imperfect and flowing from other people's insecurities rather than from a place of unconditional love. This is not always the case, of course – there are exceptional circumstances and hopefully at least one of these exceptions in every life – but it is better by far to draw your love from a cosmic source.

Religions with mother Goddesses know how to generate this perpetual feeling of being loved. Paramahansa Yogananda makes much of the Divine Mother in his writings *(see Recommended Reading)* and indeed Hinduism is very much centred around these divine sources of unconditional love. These are exactly the wavelengths that keep us healthy psychologically and whose effects may therefore be witnessed and felt on the physical level too. To know that one is loved always, that death itself is no threat and that one will always be a child of the Great Mother is a wonderful spiritual revelation indeed. It has the additional benefit of keeping us looking and feeling young.

So, to facilitate this, approach the Goddess. Images are easily available (postcards of Hindu mother Goddesses, for example) and act as excellent doorways to the deity concerned.

Another way to approach the all-giving Mother, which will be much appreciated as it involves the process of creation itself, so dear to her, is to paint or make an image of the Goddess aspect you most wish to approach. While you are doing this, you can really focus on your child aspects, the love you feel for the Cosmic Mother and on your desire to remain always in her jurisdiction and care.

The key to this youthful thinking is the sense of faith. So invest your painting or statue with that too.

When you have finished, place your Goddess image on your altar or in another place of significance to you and present it with flowers, incense, cakes and any other offerings you feel she would like.

Whenever you have need of anything ('and better it be when the Moon is full', as 'The Charge of the Goddess' puts it), approach your Goddess and talk to her. Ask her for what you need. See her as your link to the sustaining, cosmic divine, the source of all sustenance and care. You will soon find yourself feeling far more like an eternally-grateful child than a care-ridden and ageing adult.

Approach Life As If It Were an Adventure Playground

See every day as living metaphysics, filled with magickal clues to your purpose in this life. Curiosity is an enchantment in itself and keeps the spirit and body young and optimistic.

Do Not Take on Responsibilities Automatically or Because You Think You Ought

It is shocking how many people load themselves up with responsibilities just because they think they should – even getting married and having children automatically, for example, curtailing their own freedom before they have even seen anything of the world.

Live first! Travel! Nurture a sense of wonder (*not* of a 'been there and done that' nature – rather of a 'So much variety in the world, so much to see and do!' sort). And don't forget, it is never too late. We can learn new skills at any age. Many people, because they have spent the first parts of their lives performing these 'obligatory' tasks, do not learn to live their own lives until they reach their mid-fifties or sixties. It is then that they write their novel, learn to ice-skate, start to travel rather than to go on vacuum-packed family package holidays, or even learn to drive, as in the case of my own granny, when she was 65!

But whatever age you are, remember this is *your* incarnation. This does not mean being selfish and thoughtless of others, but the realization does empower you to make better decisions at crucial times. Follow your heart and spirit! This is another of the keys to eternal youth.

Experiment and Aspire

The people who live longest and most happily almost invariably have aspirations. New topics, new hobbies and new skills are all key to staying youthful.

However, beware the mentality of just desiring one particular aim, such as seeing the Egyptian pyramids – attaining a single life-long aspiration often leads to dropping dead! Essentially, the mind has been programmed to believe it has now attained everything. Make sure there is always something greater in your life to aim for.

Stay in Touch with Your Sexuality

Allow yourself to find other people attractive, even if you do not do anything about it. The hormones produced by sexual attraction (and sex) work wonders on all levels of the body and soul.

 ## Youth Revisited Visualization

This simple but effective visualization is employed by those who wish to reverse the ageing process. I first read of it in Olga Kharitidi's book on Siberian shamanism, *Entering the Circle (see Recommended Reading)*, but have discovered it in operation elsewhere since. I have also employed it to some effect myself.

- *Simply sit in meditative posture and, using your mind as a cinema-screen, envisage your face up large, in close-up.*

- *Now, age your face backwards. Gradually visualize your face regaining its looks of three years ago, five, eight, ten.*

- *Continue right back into your teens, your childhood and your infancy.*

The woman mentioned in Olga Kharitidi's book continued to visualize back to being a baby and apparently performed this exercise daily. Kharitidi relates that the woman looked literally decades younger than she actually was.

WORKING WITH THE CHAKRAS – SHAMANIC TECHNIQUES FOR ALTERING THE BODY SHAPE

As we have already mentioned, the body is surrounded by an invisible (to normal vision) electrical field, often called the aura or auric body. In some shamanic practices, the aura of a specific animal is adopted and the shaman 'becomes' the bird of prey, jaguar or wolf they are attuning to. This enables the enactment of ritual battles on the astral plane, which are sometimes echoed in the gestures of the shaman on the physical level. A similar technique may be used to refine the appearance of the body – and not simply for slimming purposes! It may be used to increase beauty, glamour, athleticism, stature and a host of other qualities.

 General Chakra Meditation

Sitting comfortably, cross-legged or in the lotus posture if you can manage it, spine straight, inhale and exhale as deeply as is comfortable for as long as you need to get relaxed and psychically attuned.

- *Start at the base chakra and visualize a wheel of delicate red light. This is usually spinning clockwise. If anything seems amiss in it, mend it. Ensure that the colour is bright and regular throughout.*

- *Next, proceed to the orange intestinal chakra. Again, check for the clarity and regularity of colour, and if anything seems 'wrong' or unusual, change it.*

- *Continue with this technique up through the yellow of the solar plexus, the emerald green of the heart chakra, the blue of the throat, the purple of the third eye and finally the brilliant white of the crown chakra.*

- Note that all of the chakras should be rotating at the same speed. If one is out of synch with the others, try to adjust it. It might help to place the palm of your hand over a chakra which you know to be healthy and the palm of the other hand on the chakra which is too fast or slow until the latter is re-adjusted. If this is not possible, get somebody else to re-align them for you, preferably a trained or proficient practitioner of the psychic arts.

- Once you have finished, stand up, stretch and place your left foot in front of your right and your left hand under your right at the solar plexus to seal your aura.

- Now assess what you encountered at each major chakra. It might help to write this down.

If it was the first time you attempted to cleanse or adjust your chakras, you may have discovered many irregularities. Even so, it is worth writing your impressions down for future reference. Recurrent impressions may indicate more permanent issues such as physical problems or unresolved emotional issues. If, for example, every time you reach your solar plexus and heart chakras you discover that they are leaking or otherwise compromised, you can begin to look at possible causes, either relating to physical issues, such as diet and the health of your heart, or to emotional issues concerning past relationships and the damage they may still be doing you. As with Magick, always look at the symbolism of what you see. It is amazing what your subconscious can tell you when you are willing to see the signs.

Regular cleansing of the chakras keeps the aura supple and thus easier to manipulate. By following this exercise regularly, you will find it much easier to project the body-image you most desire into a responsive vessel. This works in a similar way to the legendary witch's 'glamour' in which a 'hag' disguises herself as a seductive young girl. Essentially, the witch has projected her desired appearance into her etheric and astral bodies with such force that she has 'become' it on the physical level too. This technique is prevalent in shamanism and Witchcraft.

Ritual salt baths with this kind of meditation are of immense value.

 ### Chakric Slimming/Appearance-Defining Exercise

Perform this ritual any time, though evening is best. If possible, do it when there is no external light. Take some candles into the bathroom and work by their transformative magickal light instead.

- Take a handful of salt (Dead Sea salt is my personal favourite; it also smells of the ocean). Hold it to the East and focus on words to the effect of: 'O Thou, that givest Life and Form to the Universe, bless this salt that it may dissolve old habits, cleanse me and give me the power of creation over my own form.'

- As you do this, envisage a stream of brilliant orange light hitting the salt from the East and being absorbed into it.

- Run a bath. This should be neither hot nor cold, but comfortably warm. As you run the cold tap, place the salt in the stream and watch it spread orange light throughout the water. By the time you get in, your inner eye should perceive the water to be glowing with luminous, magickal light.

- As you submerge yourself in the water, imagine it dissolving your old etheric body – the old template of your body form. You could leave the features you're happy with if you wish or dissolve your 'image' in its entirely.

- Now, by the transforming light in your bathroom, look down at your body and strongly project an image of the way you would like to look over it. Visualize your stronger, more magickal, more svelte self as your own body, until you can totally see it.

- When it is solid in your mind's eye, say; 'As I Will, So Mote It Be.'

- Arise and empty the tub.

- Repeat this exercise as often as possible.

Essentially, this technique programmes your bodies etheric and physical (they follow suit) to grow a certain way – the way you want them to. The more you imprint the right image on the ether, the stronger the 'glamour' and the eventual physical effects will be.

This exercise can also be used for rejuvenation, for shamanic attuning to the powers of certain animals, for healing scars and so forth.

You might like to add oils specific to the purpose (rose for rejuvenation and beauty, orange for strength and energy, pine for healing, etc), and even solarized or colour-treated water (see Glossary) to the bath. The process can be as simple or as ritualized as you want it to be.

ATTUNING ONESELF TO NATURE

Some witches say that it is best, at least prior to ritual or a major Sabbat, to consume only those foodstuffs that are native to one's country. This makes perfect sense when the aim is to attune oneself to the energies of the environment and its configurations. Likewise, depending on which system appeals to you most, it is possible to tune the etheric/ pranic body in to that system.

For example, if you decide that a good technique for you is to work with mantras to help you slim with Spirit, you might wish to concentrate on Indian foods and ingredients. If you are working on a complementary exercise pattern (which is obviously a great aid both to slimming and to general health!), especially if it includes such techniques as running or swimming in the sea (both great for *prana*-absorption), then native foods may be best.

It is always a good thing to be aware of the country from which one's food comes and of the vibrations which are invested in it as a result. The foods which hold the most *prana* are those which have been drenched in sunlight or in one of the elements – Earth and Water being the most obvious. When fire is added to the equation, through the process of heating and cooking, we have a truly balanced meal, elementally speaking. Add to this the element of Spirit, through conscious effort and awareness, and we are consuming foods which nourish all of our bodies – physical, astral and etheric.

These processes are greatly aided by attuning to nature via walks, looking at the night sky, appreciating flowers and trees and birds, and by feeling the flow of the seasons – all good healthy ways to stay physically and magickally spry.

So, it is possible to be a priestess of Venus, as well as a priestess of other deities and paths, simply by enjoying and enhancing one's physicality and sensuality. The body is, after all, one of the many gifts of the Goddess, and if it is aligned with our Magickal and Higher Selves, all the better.

Ideally, the priestess is at home on all of these levels and can synchronize them in a way that is of optimum benefit to herself and the deities she is representing and serving.

The Nocturnal Priestess

Many of the techniques discussed in this book may be utilized by the working priestess, by which I mean the priestess who also holds down a regular job. Indeed, this is one of the reasons why I thought it meet to include so many luxurious Venusian techniques as a necessary anti-dote to the nine-to-five blues.

There are many other ways of ensuring that you stay as closely attuned to the Goddess as possible. The use of your altar for daily devo-tion, however brief, is psychologically and spiritually helpful. Lighting a candle creates an instant rapport with the deity to whom you devote the action. You can heighten the magickal vibrations by dabbing your-self with consecrated oil, such as a suitable scent – for example, I use Mercury oil when my day requires me to be super-articulate and a scent dedicated to the Muses for creativity such as writing and paint-ing. Of course, a mantra repeated before your altar before work will set your mind on a certain wavelength for the day, as will the recital of a prayer or paean.

When you get in after your day's exertions, a ritual bath will help relax both body and soul, as previously discussed. Before you go to sleep, a period of meditation may help unlock the gates to the astral levels during dreamtime. Before bed is also the ideal time to contemplate symbols and travel into them in order to unlock their inner meanings. One of the ways I became expert in Tarot analysis was by entering into the pictures in the cards in a state of drowsiness and exploring the scenes that rose before my inner eye. Contemplating such an image while drifting into semi-consciousness is a perfect way to perceive its inner meanings. One can peek behind corners and lift the veil of one-dimensionality from the image.

A technique taught in magickal training involves 'day reversal' on the brink of sleep. After settling down, the magickian, witch or priestess (actual or potential) recalls the day in detail from beginning to end. Not only does this serve to highlight the day's most relevant points, but it acts as an exercise for the memory.

This technique also creates a certain mental wavelength which is highly conducive to dreaming, particularly symbolic dreaming. Why exactly this is I cannot claim to know; I only know that it works, just as tuning in a radio brings through certain wavelengths.

There are more specific processes which may be used by the priestess. If you are working with a particular Goddess for example, why not research (or maybe remember) the layout of her temple of old and make a journey down the path towards it before you shift into dreams? When you read the novel *Moon Magic* by Dion Fortune *(see Recommended Reading)*, you will witness the heroine, Lilith Morgan Le Fay, utilizing a very similar pathworking in order to attune to her priestess-self of both past and present.

Visiting the Dream Temple of Isis Exercise

The Moon is hanging low and full in a deep blue, almost indigo sky. Constellations are scattered across the sky, their shapes familiar to you but their meanings not yet revealed. Observe them, but do not attempt to crack their codes just yet.

- *You are standing barefoot and lightly robed at the top of an avenue of tall trees, the cool, slightly moist earth sending up its pleasing scent. You feel propelled towards the hidden light you know is emanating from the temple at the end of the avenue.*

- *You begin to walk down the path, dipping your bare feet into the slanting moonshine and shadow.*

- *Tall trees flank you, their branches like dark wings, the sharp smell of cypress occasionally scintillating your senses. It feels cool and cleansing.*

- *The path is long, and as you tread it, you fall into a regular pace, a meditative rhythm.*

- *You cross a courtyard with lotus imagery carved into its pillars, and a lake, silver and oil-dark, on which float lotus flowers on their circular pads, white blossoms closed and flowering towards the Moon. A sense of 'super-nature' fills the air, intoxicating and elevating.*

- *You reach the Temple of Isis, and enter.*

- *The lamp burns above you, shedding its Perpetual Light on the black curtain before you, shielding the Holiest of Holies.*

- *You are surrounded by symbols of the Zodiac and you perceive yourself as both large and small in the schemes of the Universe.*

- *This is the place to meditate.*

- *There is no need to leave the temple unless you wish to. Isis is giver of dreams and visions, and to 'sleep' in her temple is potentially enlightening.*

You can of course change this visualization into a journey to the temple of any deity with whom you wish to work.

Glossary

Here is a glossary of the words and phrases marked * in the text.

Abra-Melin the Mage   A fifteenth-century magician whose system of magical invocations was adopted and adapted by a mystic who met Abra-Melin whilst travelling in Egypt. This mystic's name was Abraham the Jew. The result is a manuscript containing a system for attaining knowledge and conversation with one's Holy Guardian Angel and for gaining control over the demonic entities (under the rule of the Four Great Princes of Evil of the world). The work of Abra-Melin and Abraham the Jew provides us with a classic example of negative theology, characteristic of the medieval grimoires *(see below)*: one does God's work by working with the demons.

The one-time obscure system of Abra-Melin's Magick was translated by Samuel MacGregor Mathers in the nineteenth century. Mathers was the head of the Golden Dawn *(see below)*, an occult school which hugely influenced modern metaphysical practice and which produced some of the world's finest priestesses.

Assiah A Qabalistic term *(see below)* referring to the World of Matter, as opposed to that of the Divine, of Creation and of Formation. In other words, Assiah is the level of the Qabalistic spiritual system which we as humans inhabit. It is the lowest of four levels of reality, the three above being Yetzirah, Briah and Atziluth.

Atziluth A Qabalistic term *(see below)* referring to the highest spiritual realm within the Jewish mystical system which it is possible for us to contemplate. It is known variously as the Archetypal World and the World of Emanations. It is the highest of four levels of reality, the three below being Briah, Yetzirah and Assiah.

Beltane The fire-festival celebrated by the Celts on 1 May, Beltane is a celebration and invocation of fertility and regeneration. *(See 'The Wheel of Life', page 93.)*

Bhakti A Hindu term meaning 'devotional worship'. An example is the placing of flowers before the image of a deity or the performance of tasks of devotion such as the repetition of mantras of adoration.

Briah A Qabalistic term *(see below)* referring to the World of Creation. It is the second of four levels of reality, coming between Atziluth and Yetzirah, with Assiah beneath that.

Chaos Magick Chaos Magick is a modern form of magickal practice based upon the teachings of Austin Osman Spare *(see below)* and combined with the modern metascience of chaos theory and quantum mechanics. Unlike many other traditions, it has no philosophy as such; rather, it forms a flexible means of practice which can be adapted according to the Will of the user. A slogan that almost defines these methods is 'Nothing is True, Everything is Permitted' and as such it can be seen as devoid of ethics, morality and, in some practices, Karma.

Charge of the Goddess, The In Wiccan practice, after the priestess has taken the Goddess into herself and become Her living representative, she hopes to become oracular. If, however, words do not flow easily, there is a poetic oration to which she can resort, known as 'The Charge of the Goddess'. This rather beautiful declaration (written in modern form by Doreen Valiente) runs as follows:

Listen to the words of the Great Mother, who of old was also called Artemis, Astarte, Athena, Diana, Melusine, Aphrodite, Cerridwen, Dana, Arianrhod, Isis, Brid, and many other names:

Whenever you have need of anything, and better it be when the Moon is full, then shall ye assemble in some secret place and adore the spirit of Me Who am Queen of all Witches. There shall ye assemble, ye who are fain to learn all sorcery, yet have not won its deepest secrets; to these I will teach things that are yet unknown.

And ye shall be free from slavery, and as a sign that ye be really free, ye shall be naked in your rites; and ye shall dance, sing, feast, make music and love, all in My praise. For Mine is the ecstasy of the spirit and Mine is also joy on earth. For My Law is Love unto all beings. For Mine is the secret door that opens upon the land of youth, and Mine is the cup of the wine of Life, and the cauldron of Cerridwen that is the holy grail of immortality. I am the gracious Goddess, who gives the gift of joy unto all hearts.

Upon Earth, I give the knowledge of the spirit eternal; and beyond death I give peace and freedom and reunion with those that have gone before. Nor do I demand aught of sacrifice, for behold, I am the Mother of all things and My Love is poured out upon the earth.

Hear ye the words of the Star Goddess, she in the dust of Whose Feet are the Hosts of Heaven, and whose body encircles the Universe:

I Who am the beauty of the green Earth and the white Moon among the stars and the Mysteries of the waters, and the desire of all hearts, call unto thy soul. Arise and come with Me. For I am the soul of nature who gives life unto the Universe. From Me all things proceed, and Unto Me all things must return; and before my face, beloved of Gods and of men, let thine innermost divine self be enfolded in the rapture of the Infinite.

Let My worship be within the heart that rejoices, for behold, all acts of Love and pleasure are My rituals. And therefore let there be beauty and strength, power and compassion, honour and humility, mirth and reverence within you.

And thou who thinkest to seek for Me, know thy seeking and yearning shall avail thee not, unless thou knowest the Mystery: for if that which thou seekest, thou findest not within, then thou shalt never find it without. For behold, I have been with thee from the beginning, and I am that which is attained at the end of desire.

Circle, casting The Circle is the protected space in which witches and other practitioners of the esoteric arts work. In actual fact it is a sphere psychically and astrally speaking, but it is 'cast' in the form of a circle, with the practitioner at the centre. The elements are invoked, or various entities as required, and protection is asked for. Work is not started until the space is secure.

The Circle is usually ritualistically 'opened' after these processes are completed, though sometimes it is left as is. The circumference of the Circle is not crossed until protection is no longer required.

Golden Dawn, the A groundbreaking occult group founded in 1887, school to many of our finest modern priestesses. *(See Chapter 2.)*

Grant, Kenneth A practitioner of what is known as 'Typhonian' Magick. This refers to a particular tradition of Ancient Egypt which placed great emphasis on the Goddess Typhon (symbolized by the stars of Ursa Major), later suppressed by the solar logos. Grant has written many excellent books on the darker side of ultra-modern Magick, including much about the role of the priestess *(see Recommended Reading)*.

Great Voice This is the inner voice which is clearly directed, as opposed to simple rambling thoughts. For example, in ritual one is entirely focused on the work to hand. Thus, even if the outer voice is not utilized, the Great Voice will sound to the inner ear exactly as it would if one were orating aloud. The idea is that the Great Voice is audible on several levels and is certainly not confined to one's own head. It has the advantage, however, of not being audible to house-mates and neighbours, and thus is particularly well suited to modern and particularly urban living.

Grimoire Meaning 'grammar' and essentially referring to a book of rules and regulations, this has now become a term referring to a magickal handbook, particularly a medieval one. For example, *The Book of the Sacred Magic of Abra-Melin the Mage (see above)* is a grimoire.

Isian Era In Ancient Egypt, the Isian Era or Age of Isis followed the Age of Ra. Ra was a Sun God, masculine in nature. Isis is of course feminine and lunar. Her popularity overtook that of Ra; in mythological terms, this was when Isis tricked Ra into telling her his sacred name (or personal vibration), thus giving her control over him.

Malkuth The lowest sephirah *(see below)* on the Qabalistic Tree of Life. Malkuth in its lowest aspect (in Assiah, *see above*) represents the level which we inhabit as humans in the mystical cosmos.

Mather, Cotton A Boston minister who initiated the seventeenth-century witch hunts, including the famed Salem witch trials.

Maya A Sanskrit word meaning 'illusion', referring to the fact that physical matter is an illusion which disguises the spiritual energies which create it. Understanding of *Maya* reveals that death is also an illusion.

O.T.O. The letters O.T.O. stand for Ordo Templi Orientis, which means the Order of the Temple of the East. It was founded in 1895 by high-ranking continental Freemasons, Tantricks and Gnostic adepts, and like the Golden Dawn differed from regular Freemasonry by incorporating magickal work into its curriculum and also by admitting women as well as men into its ranks. The Order itself is best characterized by schism and today there are several variant groups and philosophies active. These include the Typhonian O.T.O. and Albion O.T.O. in Britain, the Swiss O.T.O. in Europe and the Society O.T.O. in America and Australia.

Powers of the Sphinx In the esoteric arts, the Powers of the Sphinx are analogous to those of the effective practitioner of Magick. They may be summarized as follows: to Know, to Will, to Dare and to Be Silent. Crowley adds one more: to Go. The latter adds dynamism to the equation.

Qabalah A Jewish mystical system adapted by the Western Mystery Tradition *(see below)* into a working magickal format. Qabalah is thus not the same as Kabbalah, the original medieval Jewish system which has recently become so popular, nor is it the same as Cabala, the Christianized version. The Golden Dawn *(see above)* was largely responsible for Qabalah, using the original system as part of its highly eclectic magickal studies and explorations. Qabalah is now key to esoteric studies as various as those found in Wicca and the Society of the Inner Light *(both outlined below)*.

Sephiroth/Sephirah The Qabalistic Tree of Life includes 10 spheres, or sephirah, each representative of a different set of qualities. These are too complex to outline here, but a glance at any diagram of the Qabalah *(see above)* will be self-explanatory.

Shakti The divine female principle in the Cosmic Whole, the consort and complementary opposite to the divine male principle Siva, the Shakti is the principle which moves and creates a dynamic.

Society of the Inner Light, the The Society of the Inner Light (SIL) is a Mystery School within the Western Esoteric Tradition, founded by Dion Fortune *(see Chapter 2)*. It offers courses in its interpretations of this major priestess's work. These are also available (in a different format) from the Servants of the Light, a splinter group of the SIL.

Solarization The exposure of liquids, gems and so on to sunlight in order to charge them with solar qualities. Lunarization is the nocturnal equivalent, in which substances and objects are endowed with the energies and properties of the lunar currents.

Spare, Austin Osman Born in 1886, Austin Osman Spare was an expert draftsman and artist by the time he was 18 and his interest in the occult was already pronounced. Fêted at an early age and offered a life of adulation and opulence, he turned his back on 'high' society and instead dedicated himself to a life of experimental Magick, much of which is recorded in his artwork.

Synaesthesia The ability to hear colour, smell sound, and so on. Many magickally talented people have these and similar abilities. Synaesthesia also encompasses the ability to visualize music and tone. This is of course a very handy trait for the artistically-inclined priestess, enabling the translation of concepts from one level to another.

Tantric Vama-Marg Current Vama Marg means 'Left-Hand Way', as opposed to the Dakshina Marg, or 'Right-Hand Way'. In Tantric tradition the left-hand is considered to be the female or lunar path, in contrast to the right-hand, male or solar path. The main focus of its rites centres on one or several priestesses that are considered divine embodiments of the Goddess. It also utilizes the physical rites and elixirs that can be generated. This led to it being generally shunned and suppressed by Eastern society in general.

Thelema The school of magickal practice set up by Aleister Crowley. The word 'Thelema' means 'Will'; the idea is to follow one's Higher Will. This involves immense focus and dedication, as the aim is spiritual evolution and the reining in (rather than abnegation) of the physical and emotional responses.

Theosophy The school of spiritual philosophy initiated by Helena Blavatsky, one of our most potent and influential modern priestesses.

Theosophy hugely influenced the Golden Dawn *(see above)*, modern Wicca *(see below)* and many other systems of esoteric study. It introduced a great deal of Eastern terminology and concept into Western esoteric lore, and the idea of 'Hidden Masters', or ascended souls whose desire and role is to aid humanity in its evolution. One of the aims of the Theosophist is to be in contact on the inner planes with such elevated beings.

Western Mystery Tradition The legacy of the many spiritual and mystical paths in the Occident. Used in this book to refer particularly to the work of groups such as the Golden Dawn *(see above)*.

Wicca A modern version of Witchcraft practice, Wicca falls into many sub-divisions, but most of these are ramifications of two main versions, known as Alexandrian and Gardenarian, after their founders, Alex Sanders and Gerald Gardner.

Wicca is usually construed to be a religion of nature-worship, and certainly the 'Sabbats' around which the Wiccan year rotates are Celtic agricultural festivals. However, in many cases this basic Paganism has become intertwined with aspects of High Magick and spell-casting, producing a series of beliefs and techniques as eclectic and idiosyncratic as its practitioners.

Witch's Pyramid Some people see this as a witch's version of the Powers of the Sphinx *(see above)*, but with 'To Imagine' instead of 'To Go'. In other terminology it is a spell or incantation which repeats and diminishes in accordance with the aim of the exercise.

Yesod In Qabalah *(see above)*, Yesod is the sephirah *(see above)* above Malkuth *(see above)*, representing the Astral Sphere. Yesod is the area of imagination, emotion and glamour.

Young, Ella Fenian activist who, like her friend Maud Gonne, had a profound interest in re-activating Irish folklore and mythology.

Recommended Reading

Please note this list is far from comprehensive. It is only possible to mention a tiny proportion of the books which influenced or are mentioned in this one.

Beckman, Howard, *Mantras, Yantras and Fabulous Gems*, Balaji Publishing Co., USA, 1997

Brennan, Barbara Ann, *Hands of Light*, Bantam, New York, USA, 1988

Chopra, Deepak, *Ageless Body, Timeless Mind*, Rider, London, UK, 1993

Clark, Rosemary, *The Sacred Magic of Ancient Egypt*, Llewellyn Publications, St Paul, Minnesota, USA, 2003

Dali, Salvador, *Hidden Faces*, Peter Owen Ltd, London, UK, 1973

Edwards, Gill, *Stepping into the Magic*, Piatkus, London, UK, 1993

Fortune, Dion: All of Dion Fortune's books are highly recommended, especially *The Winged Bull, The Goat Foot God, Secrets of Dr*

Taverner, The Demon Lover, The Sea Priestess and *Moon Magic*. All of her books are available from The Society of the Inner Light, 38 Steele's Road, London NW3 4RG, UK.

Gawain, Shakti, *Creative Visualisation*, Bantam Press, New York, USA, 1983

Grant, Kenneth, *Hecate's Fountain*, Skoob Books Publishing Ltd, London, UK, 1990

–, *The Magical Revival*, Skoob Books Publishing Ltd, London, UK, 1991

–, *Nightside of Eden*, Skoob Books Ltd, London, UK, 1994

Graves, Robert, *The White Goddess*, Faber and Faber Ltd, London, UK, 1953

Greer, Mary K., *Women of the Golden Dawn: Rebels and Priestesses*, Park Street Press, Rochester, Vermont, USA, 1995

Hall, Judy, *The Crystal Bible*, Godsfield Press Ltd, London, UK, 2003

Harris, Nathaniel J., *Witcha: A Book of Cunning*, Mandrake of Oxford, UK, 2004

Hay, Louise, *You Can Heal Your Life*, Hay House Inc., Santa Monica, CA, USA, 1988

Heath, Maya, *Handbook of Incense, Oils, and Candles*, Words of Wizdom International, Texas, USA, 1996

Kharitidi, Olga, *Entering the Circle*, Thorsons, London, UK, 1997

Kinsley, David, *The Goddesses' Mirror*, State University of New York Press, Albany, USA, 1989

Lemesurier, Peter, *The Healing of the Gods*, Element Books, Dorset, UK, 1988

Peach, Emily, *Tarot Prediction*, The Aquarian Press, Wellingborough, UK, 1988

Nema, *Maat Magick*, Samuel Weiser, Inc., Maine, USA, 2004

Rhodes, Jewell Parker, *Voodoo Dreams*, Picador, New York, USA, 1993. A great novel about a Voodoo priestess!

Richardson, Alan, *Priestess: The Life and Magic of Dion Fortune*, The Aquarian Press, Wellingborough, UK, 1987

Robertson, Dame Olivia: The Fellowship of Isis, headed by the priestess Olivia, produces many fine books and pamphlets on Goddess history and the work of the priestess. Information may be found at www.fellowshipofisis.com.

Rose, Sharron, *The Path of the Priestess*, Inner Traditions, Rochester, Vermont, USA, 2002

Roth, Gabrielle: All of Gabrielle Roth's many books and CDs are relevant to the subject of this book.

Sharman-Burke, Juliet, *The Mythic Tarot Workbook*, Rider/Random House, London, UK, 1989

Suster, Gerald, *John Dee*, North Atlantic Books, Berkeley, California, USA, 1986

Trobe, Kala, *Invoke the Goddess*, Llewellyn Publications, St Paul, Minnesota, USA, 2000

–, *The Witch's Guide to Life*, Llewellyn Publications, St Paul, Minnesota, USA, 2003

Wills, Pauline, *Colour Therapy*, Element Books, Dorset, UK, 1993

Wishart, Catherine, *Teen Goddess: How to Look, Love and Live Like a Goddess*, Llewellyn Publications, St Paul, Minnesota, USA, 2003

Yogananda, Paramahansa, *Autobiography of a Yogi*, Self-Realization Fellowship, Los Angeles, CA, USA, 1990

Notes

Notes

Notes

Notes

Notes

Notes